Ethical Hacking

Understanding the basics of Hacking Tools and Techniques for Cybersecurity and Safeguarding Information in computer systems and computer networks

Lewis Finan

Table of Contents

Introduction

In today's interconnected world, where digital technologies play an integral role in our daily lives, ensuring the security and integrity of computer systems and networks has become paramount. With the increasing sophistication of cyber threats and the potential for devastating cyberattacks, the demand for skilled cybersecurity professionals has never been higher. Among these professionals, ethical hackers stand out as the guardians of digital security, using their knowledge and expertise to identify vulnerabilities and strengthen defenses against malicious actors.

Ethical Hacking: Understanding the Basics of Hacking Tools and Techniques for Cybersecurity and Safeguarding Information in Computer Systems and Computer Networks aims to provide a comprehensive introduction to the fascinating world of ethical hacking. This book is designed for beginners and cybersecurity enthusiasts who are keen to delve into the realm of ethical hacking and learn the tools, techniques, and methodologies used by ethical hackers to protect organizations from cyber threats.

The term 'hacking' often carries negative connotations due to its association with cybercrime and illegal activities. However, not all hacking is malicious. Ethical hacking, also known as penetration testing or white-hat hacking, refers to the practice of identifying vulnerabilities in computer systems and networks lawfully and responsibly. Ethical hackers use their skills to uncover weaknesses that could potentially be exploited by cybercriminals, allowing organizations to address these vulnerabilities proactively and enhance their security posture.

This book begins by providing a foundational understanding of computer systems, networks, and cybersecurity principles. Readers will learn about the different types of networks, common cybersecurity threats, and the fundamental principles of information security. Building on this knowledge, the book explores various hacking methodologies, including reconnaissance, scanning, and enumeration, gaining access, and maintaining access. Each chapter delves into specific hacking tools and techniques, equipping readers with practical skills and insights into the world of ethical hacking.

Throughout the book, an emphasis is placed on ethical considerations and legal compliance. Readers will gain an understanding of the ethical guidelines that govern the practice of ethical hacking and the importance of conducting penetration testing responsibly and lawfully. Additionally, the book covers the legal landscape of cybersecurity, highlighting key laws and regulations that cybersecurity professionals must be aware of to avoid legal pitfalls.

As you embark on this journey into the world of ethical hacking, you will gain valuable knowledge and skills that are highly sought after in the cybersecurity industry. Whether you are looking to pursue a career as an ethical hacker, enhance your cybersecurity expertise, or simply gain a deeper understanding of the tools and techniques used to safeguard information in computer systems and networks, this book will serve as your comprehensive guide.

Prepare to expand your horizons, challenge your thinking, and explore the exciting field of ethical hacking. Let's embark on this adventure together and take the first step towards becoming a cybersecurity defender in our increasingly digital world.

Definition and Importance of Ethical Hacking

Ethical hacking, also known as penetration testing or white-hat hacking, refers to the practice of deliberately and lawfully attempting to identify vulnerabilities in computer systems, networks, and applications. Ethical hackers use their skills, tools, and techniques to simulate cyberattacks with the explicit permission of the system owner. The primary objective of ethical hacking is to uncover weaknesses that could be exploited by malicious actors, thereby helping organizations strengthen their security defenses and protect their valuable assets from cyber threats.

Unlike malicious hacking, which aims to compromise systems for personal gain or malicious intent, ethical hacking is conducted with integrity and within legal boundaries. Ethical hackers adhere to strict ethical guidelines and professional standards, ensuring that their actions do not cause harm or damage to the target systems.

Importance of Ethical Hacking

In today's digital landscape, where cyber threats are evolving rapidly, the importance of ethical hacking cannot be overstated. Ethical hackers play a crucial role in enhancing cybersecurity by identifying and addressing vulnerabilities before they can be exploited by cybercriminals. Here are some key reasons why ethical hacking is important:

- **Proactive Security Measures**: Ethical hacking allows organizations to proactively identify and remediate vulnerabilities in their systems and networks. By conducting regular penetration tests, organizations can stay one step ahead of cyber threats and ensure that their security defenses are robust and effective.

- **Risk Mitigation**: Identifying and fixing vulnerabilities through ethical hacking helps organizations reduce the risk of data breaches, financial losses, and reputational damage. By addressing security weaknesses proactively, organizations can avoid the costly consequences of cyberattacks.

- **Compliance and Regulation**: Many industries are subject to regulatory requirements and compliance standards related to cybersecurity. Ethical hacking can help organizations demonstrate compliance with industry regulations and standards by ensuring that their systems and networks meet the necessary security requirements.

- **Enhanced Trust and Reputation**: Implementing strong cybersecurity measures, including ethical hacking, demonstrates a commitment to protecting customer data and sensitive information. This can enhance customer trust and confidence in the organization's ability to safeguard their information, leading to a positive reputation in the marketplace.

- **Skill Development and Training**: Ethical hacking provides cybersecurity professionals with valuable hands-on experience and training opportunities. By engaging in ethical hacking activities, professionals can hone their technical skills, stay updated on the latest cyber threats and trends, and develop expertise in identifying and mitigating security risks.

In conclusion, ethical hacking plays a vital role in the cybersecurity ecosystem, helping organizations identify and mitigate vulnerabilities, protect against cyber threats, and maintain a strong security posture. By embracing ethical hacking as a proactive security measure, organizations can safeguard their assets, build trust with stakeholders, and navigate the complex landscape of cybersecurity with confidence.

Ethics and Legality in Hacking

The world of hacking is often shrouded in misconceptions and stereotypes, with the term 'hacker' frequently associated with cyber criminals and illegal activities. However, not all hacking is malicious or illegal. Ethical hacking, when conducted responsibly and within legal boundaries, serves a vital role in enhancing cybersecurity and safeguarding digital assets. Understanding the ethical and legal considerations in hacking is essential for anyone involved in cybersecurity, particularly ethical hackers, to ensure that their actions are lawful, ethical, and beneficial.

Ethics in Hacking

Ethics refers to a set of moral principles that guide individuals' behavior and decision-making. In the context of hacking, ethical considerations revolve around conducting activities that are honest, responsible, and respectful toward others' rights and privacy. Here are some key ethical principles that ethical hackers should adhere to:

- **Permission**: Ethical hackers must obtain explicit permission from the system owner before conducting any penetration testing or vulnerability assessment. Unauthorized hacking, even if done with good intentions, is illegal and unethical.
- **Integrity**: Ethical hackers should act with honesty and transparency, accurately reporting their findings without exaggeration or distortion. They should prioritize the accuracy and reliability of their assessments to ensure that organizations can make informed decisions about their security posture.

- **Confidentiality**: Ethical hackers are often exposed to sensitive information during their assessments. It is crucial to handle this information with care and maintain confidentiality to protect the organization's data and privacy.
- **Respect for Others**: Ethical hackers should respect the rights and privacy of individuals and organizations. They should refrain from causing harm, disruption, or unnecessary stress during their testing activities and prioritize minimizing any potential impact on the target systems.

Legality in Hacking

While ethical hacking aims to improve cybersecurity and protect organizations from cyber threats, it must be conducted within the boundaries of the law. Engaging in unauthorized hacking or violating cybersecurity laws can lead to severe legal consequences, including fines, imprisonment, and damage to one's reputation. Here are some key legal considerations that ethical hackers should be aware of:

- **Authorization**: As mentioned earlier, ethical hackers must obtain explicit written permission from the system owner before conducting any penetration testing or vulnerability assessment. Failure to do so can result in legal repercussions.
- **Compliance with Laws and Regulations**: Ethical hackers should be familiar with the relevant cybersecurity laws, regulations, and industry standards that govern their activities. This includes understanding laws related to computer fraud, unauthorized access, data privacy, and intellectual property rights.
- **Documentation and Reporting**: Ethical hackers should maintain detailed documentation of their testing activities, methodologies,

and findings. In the event of any legal inquiries or investigations, having thorough documentation can help demonstrate that the hacking activities were conducted responsibly and within legal boundaries.

- **Responsible Disclosure**: If ethical hackers discover vulnerabilities that could potentially harm users or compromise sensitive information, they should follow responsible disclosure practices. This involves notifying the affected organization promptly and providing them with sufficient time to address and remediate the vulnerabilities before disclosing them publicly.

In conclusion, ethics and legality are integral aspects of ethical hacking, guiding the behavior and actions of ethical hackers to ensure that they contribute positively to cybersecurity without causing harm or violating laws. By adhering to ethical principles and legal requirements, ethical hackers can effectively identify and mitigate vulnerabilities, protect organizations from cyber threats, and uphold the integrity and trustworthiness of the cybersecurity profession.

Chapter 1: Understanding Computer Systems and Networks

In the bustling digital age, we find ourselves in, understanding the intricacies of computer systems and networks has become akin to understanding the inner workings of the human body. Just as our veins and arteries channel life-giving blood throughout our bodies, computer systems, and networks carry vital information, connecting us to the world and each other.

The Foundation: Computer Systems

At the heart of any computer system lies the central processing unit (CPU), often referred to as the brain of the computer. This silicon masterpiece performs millions of calculations per second, orchestrating every task the computer undertakes. But a CPU alone does not make a computer. Surrounding it are various components like memory (RAM), storage (Hard Drives or SSDs), and input/output devices such as keyboards, mice, and monitors.

Think of the CPU as the conductor of an orchestra, guiding each instrument to produce a harmonious melody. Each component plays a crucial role, in ensuring the computer functions seamlessly.

The Backbone: Computer Networks

While individual computers are powerful in their own right, their true potential is unlocked when they are connected through networks. Imagine a vast highway system where data travels at lightning speed, reaching its destination in the blink of an eye. That's the power of computer networks.

Networks come in different shapes and sizes, from local area networks (LANs) that connect devices within a limited area like a home or office, to wide area networks (WANs) that span across cities, countries, and even continents. These networks rely on various hardware devices like routers, switches, and modems to ensure data is routed efficiently to its intended destination.

The Symbiotic Relationship

Computer systems and networks share a symbiotic relationship. A computer system without a network is like a bird with clipped wings; it may function, but its ability to soar is limited. On the other hand, a network without computers is like a highway without vehicles; it exists but serves no purpose.

Together, computer systems and networks form the backbone of the digital world we inhabit, enabling us to communicate, collaborate, and create in ways our ancestors could only dream of.

The Evolving Landscape

As technology continues to advance at a breakneck pace, our understanding of computer systems and networks must evolve as well. Concepts that were cutting-edge yesterday are commonplace today, and what is considered revolutionary today may be obsolete tomorrow.

Staying abreast of these changes is crucial, not just for tech enthusiasts but for everyone who relies on technology in their daily lives. By understanding the fundamentals of computer systems and networks, we empower ourselves to navigate the digital landscape with confidence, harnessing its power to enrich our lives and shape the world around us.

In this chapter, we've scratched the surface of the fascinating world of computer systems and networks. We've explored the components that make up a computer system, delved into the intricacies of computer networks, and examined the symbiotic relationship between the two.

As we journey further into this book, we will delve deeper into these topics, exploring advanced concepts, emerging technologies, and real-world applications. Whether you're a seasoned tech veteran or a curious novice, there's something in store for everyone.

So, buckle up and get ready for an enlightening exploration of the digital realm. The adventure has just begun!

1.1 Basics of Computer Systems

The Central Processing Unit (CPU)

The Central Processing Unit, or CPU, is often described as the brain of a computer. It's responsible for executing instructions from programs stored in memory. CPUs come in various forms, with different specifications and capabilities, but they all perform the essential task of processing data.

Memory: RAM and Storage

Computers use two primary types of memory: Random Access Memory (RAM) and storage.

- **RAM (Random Access Memory)**: This is the computer's short-term memory. It stores data that the CPU needs quick access to, allowing for fast data retrieval and manipulation. However, RAM is volatile, meaning it loses its data when the computer is turned off.
- **Storage**: Unlike RAM, storage provides long-term memory for your computer. This includes Hard Disk Drives (HDDs) and Solid State Drives (SSDs). While storage is non-volatile, meaning it retains data even when the computer is turned off, it's generally slower than RAM.

Input/Output (I/O) Devices

Input and output devices allow users to interact with the computer and receive information from it.

- **Keyboards and Mice**: These are the most common input devices, allowing users to input commands and data into the computer.
- **Monitors**: The primary output device, monitors display the computer's output, including text, graphics, and videos.

Motherboard

The motherboard serves as the foundation of the computer, connecting all the components. It houses the CPU, RAM slots, and connectors for other hardware components like storage devices, graphics cards, and network cards.

Power Supply Unit (PSU)

The Power Supply Unit converts electrical power from an outlet into a form that the computer's components can use. It provides the necessary energy to keep the computer running smoothly.

Operating System (OS)

The Operating System acts as the intermediary between the user and the computer hardware. It manages the computer's resources, provides services for computer programs, and enables users to interact with the computer through a graphical user interface (GUI).

Software and Applications

Software refers to the programs and applications that run on a computer. From word processors and web browsers to games and multimedia tools, the software enables users to perform various tasks and functions on their computers.

Understanding the basics of computer systems provides a solid foundation for delving deeper into the world of technology. Each component plays a vital role in ensuring the computer's functionality, from the CPU's processing power to the storage's data retention capabilities.

As we progress through this book, we'll explore these components in greater detail, uncovering the magic that makes computers tick and the role they play in shaping our digital world. So, let's continue our journey into the fascinating realm of computer systems.

1.2 Introduction to Computer Networks

What is a Computer Network?

A computer network is a collection of computers, servers, and other devices interconnected to share resources and communicate with each other. These networks can be as simple as a few computers connected in a home or office setting, or as complex as global networks spanning continents.

Types of Computer Networks

- **Local Area Network (LAN)**

A Local Area Network, or LAN, is a network that connects devices within a limited area, such as a home, office, or school. LANs typically use Ethernet cables or Wi-Fi to connect devices and allow for the sharing of resources like printers, files, and internet connections.

- **Wide Area Network (WAN)**

A Wide Area Network, or WAN, spans a larger geographic area, often connecting LANs across cities, countries, or continents. The internet itself can be considered the largest WAN, connecting billions of devices worldwide.

- **Wireless Networks**

Wireless networks, such as Wi-Fi and cellular networks, use radio waves to transmit data without the need for physical cables. These networks offer flexibility and convenience, allowing devices to connect and communicate wirelessly within a certain range.

Network Devices

- **Routers**

Routers are essential network devices that forward data packets between different networks. They determine the best path for data to travel, ensuring efficient communication between devices.

- **Switches**

Switches are devices that connect devices within a network, allowing them to communicate with each other. Unlike routers, switches operate at the data link layer (Layer 2) of the OSI model and are essential for creating and managing LANs.

- **Modems**

Modems connect a network to the internet, translating digital data from your network into a format that can be transmitted over a communication line, such as a phone line or cable connection.

- **Network Protocols**

Network protocols are sets of rules and conventions that govern how data is transmitted and received over a network. Some common protocols include:

- **TCP/IP**: The Transmission Control Protocol/Internet Protocol is the foundational protocol of the internet, responsible for routing data packets across networks.
- **HTTP/HTTPS**: HyperText Transfer Protocol and its secure version, HTTPS, are protocols used for transmitting web pages over the internet.
- **FTP**: File Transfer Protocol is used for transferring files between a client and a server on a network.

Computer networks form the backbone of our interconnected world, enabling communication, collaboration, and resource sharing on a global scale. Understanding the basics of computer networks, from the types of networks and devices to the protocols that govern them, is essential for anyone navigating the digital landscape.

As we delve deeper into this book, we'll explore the intricacies of networking, uncovering how data travels across networks, the challenges of network security, and the innovations driving the future of networking.

So, let's continue our exploration of the fascinating world of computer networks and discover the magic that connects us all!

1.3 Types of Networks: LAN, WAN, and VPN

Local Area Network (LAN)

A Local Area Network (LAN) is a network that connects devices within a limited geographical area, such as a home, office building, or campus. LANs are commonly used to facilitate communication and resource sharing among computers and other devices.

Characteristics of LAN:

- **Limited Geographic Area**: LANs typically cover a small area, such as a single building or a group of buildings.
- **High Data Transfer Rates**: Due to their limited size, LANs often offer high-speed data transfer rates, making them ideal for tasks that require quick access to shared resources.
- **Ethernet or Wi-Fi Connectivity**: LANs commonly use Ethernet cables or Wi-Fi technology to connect devices to the network.

Wide Area Network (WAN)

A Wide Area Network (WAN) spans a larger geographical area, connecting multiple LANs and other networks across cities, countries, or even continents. The internet itself is the most prominent example of a WAN, connecting billions of devices worldwide.

Characteristics of WAN:

- **Large Geographic Area**: WANs can cover vast distances, connecting devices across different cities, countries, or continents
- **Lower Data Transfer Rates**: Due to the extended distances involved, WANs typically offer lower data transfer rates compared to LANs.
- **Utilizes Public and Private Networks**: WANs can operate over public networks, like the internet, or private networks established by organizations.

Virtual Private Network (VPN)

A Virtual Private Network (VPN) extends a private network across a public network, enabling users to send and receive data as if their devices were directly connected to a private network. VPNs are commonly used to enhance security and privacy when accessing the internet.

Characteristics of VPN:

- **Secure Data Transmission**: VPNs encrypt data to ensure secure transmission over public networks, protecting sensitive information from unauthorized access.
- **Anonymity and Privacy**: By masking your IP address, VPNs offer a level of anonymity and privacy, making it more difficult for third parties to track your online activities.
- **Remote Access**: VPNs allow remote users to access resources on a private network securely, making them ideal for remote work and accessing geographically restricted content.

Understanding the different types of networks, including LANs, WANs, and VPNs, is essential for grasping the complexities of modern-day communication and connectivity. Each type of network serves a unique purpose, catering to specific needs and requirements.

- LANs facilitate communication and resource sharing within a confined area, offering high-speed connectivity for local tasks.
- WANs connect multiple LANs and networks across vast distances, enabling global communication and access to remote resources.
- VPNs provide secure and private access to public networks, enhancing security and anonymity for users accessing the internet.

As we delve deeper into the world of networking, we'll explore how these networks interact, the technologies that power them, and the best practices for designing and managing them effectively.

Chapter 2: Fundamentals of Cybersecurity

In today's interconnected world, cybersecurity has become a cornerstone of our digital lives. As we rely more on technology for communication, work, and entertainment, the need to protect our data and privacy from cyber threats has never been greater. This chapter delves into the fundamentals of cybersecurity, exploring the principles, threats, and practices that safeguard our digital assets.

What is Cybersecurity?

Cybersecurity refers to the practice of protecting computer systems, networks, and data from theft, damage, or unauthorized access. It encompasses a range of strategies, technologies, and practices designed to safeguard information and ensure the integrity, confidentiality, and availability of digital assets.

The Pillars of Cybersecurity

- **Confidentiality**

Confidentiality ensures that data is accessible only to authorized individuals or systems. Encryption plays a crucial role in maintaining confidentiality by converting data into a coded format that can only be decoded by authorized parties.

- **Integrity**

Integrity ensures that data remains unchanged and uncorrupted during storage, transmission, and processing. Techniques like checksums and digital signatures help detect and prevent unauthorized alterations to data.

- **Availability**

Availability ensures that systems and data are accessible when needed. Redundancy, backups, and disaster recovery plans are essential components of ensuring availability, minimizing downtime, and ensuring business continuity.

Common Cyber Threats

- **Malware**

Malware, short for malicious software, encompasses a variety of malicious programs designed to damage, disrupt, or gain unauthorized access to computer systems. Common types of malware include viruses, worms, Trojans, and ransomware.

- **Phishing**

Phishing attacks involve fraudulent attempts to obtain sensitive information, such as usernames, passwords, and credit card details, by disguising it as a trustworthy entity in electronic communication.

- **Denial of Service (DoS) Attacks**

DoS attacks aim to overwhelm a system or network with excessive traffic, causing it to become slow, unresponsive, or unavailable to legitimate users.

Cybersecurity Best Practices

- **Strong Passwords**

Creating strong, unique passwords and changing them regularly is essential for protecting accounts and preventing unauthorized access.

- **Multi-factor Authentication (MFA)**

MFA adds an extra layer of security by requiring users to provide multiple forms of identification before granting access to accounts or systems.

- **Regular Updates and Patch Management**

Keeping software, operating systems, and applications up to date with the latest security patches helps protect against known vulnerabilities and exploits.

- **Security Awareness Training**

Educating employees and users about cybersecurity risks, best practices, and how to recognize and respond to threats is crucial for maintaining a strong security posture.

Cybersecurity is a complex and evolving field that plays a vital role in protecting our digital world. Understanding the fundamentals of cybersecurity, from the principles of confidentiality, integrity, and availability to the common threats and best practices, is essential for anyone navigating the digital landscape.

As we continue to embrace technology in our daily lives, the importance of cybersecurity cannot be overstated. By implementing robust security measures, staying informed about emerging threats, and adopting a proactive approach to cybersecurity, we can protect our digital assets and enjoy a safer, more secure online experience.

In the following chapters, we will delve deeper into specific cybersecurity topics, exploring advanced concepts, tools, and strategies to help you build and maintain a resilient cybersecurity posture. So, let's continue our journey into the fascinating world of cybersecurity and empower ourselves to navigate the digital realm securely!

2.1 Importance of Cybersecurity

In an era where digital transformation is reshaping industries, economies, and societies, the importance of cybersecurity has never been more critical. As we integrate technology into every aspect of our lives, from banking and healthcare to entertainment and communication, the risks associated with cyber threats continue to escalate. This section highlights the significance of cybersecurity and its role in safeguarding our digital ecosystem.

Protection of Sensitive Information

One of the primary reasons cybersecurity is essential is the protection of sensitive information. Personal data, financial records, intellectual property, and confidential communications are valuable assets that, if compromised, can lead to identity theft, financial loss, reputational damage, and legal consequences. Implementing robust cybersecurity measures helps safeguard these assets, ensuring they remain confidential and secure.

Preservation of Privacy

In today's interconnected world, maintaining privacy online has become increasingly challenging. Cybersecurity measures, such as encryption, secure communication protocols, and privacy controls, help protect individuals' privacy by preventing unauthorized access to personal information and ensuring that data is handled responsibly and ethically.

Business Continuity and Resilience

For businesses, cybersecurity is not just a matter of protecting data; it's about ensuring business continuity and resilience. Cyberattacks can disrupt operations, halt production, and lead to significant financial losses. By investing in cybersecurity, organizations can mitigate risks, minimize downtime, and maintain business continuity, safeguarding their reputation and ensuring long-term success.

Trust and Confidence in Digital Services

Trust is the cornerstone of the digital economy. Consumers, businesses, and governments must have confidence in the security and reliability of digital services and platforms. Effective cybersecurity practices build trust by demonstrating a commitment to protecting users' data and providing a secure environment for online interactions, transactions, and communications.

Compliance and Regulatory Requirements

As cyber threats continue to evolve, governments and regulatory bodies worldwide are implementing stringent cybersecurity regulations and standards to protect citizens and organizations. Compliance with these requirements is not only a legal obligation but also a testament to an organization's commitment to cybersecurity best practices. Failure to comply can result in fines, penalties, and damage to an organization's reputation.

The importance of cybersecurity extends far beyond protecting data; it's about safeguarding our digital way of life. Whether you're an individual, a business, or a government entity, cybersecurity plays a vital role in ensuring the integrity, confidentiality, and availability of digital assets and services.

As we navigate the complexities of the digital age, embracing a proactive approach to cybersecurity is crucial. By investing in robust security measures, staying informed about emerging threats, and fostering a culture of security awareness and responsibility, we can create a safer, more secure digital ecosystem for everyone.

In the upcoming chapters, we will explore the various aspects of cybersecurity in greater detail, providing insights, strategies, and practical tips to help you build and maintain a resilient cybersecurity posture. So, let's continue our exploration of the fascinating world of cybersecurity and empower ourselves to thrive in the digital age securely!

2.2 Threats, Vulnerabilities, and Attacks

Understanding the landscape of cybersecurity requires us to delve into the concepts of threats, vulnerabilities, and attacks. These terms form the foundation of cybersecurity risk assessment and management, helping organizations and individuals identify, evaluate, and mitigate potential risks to their digital assets. In this section, we'll explore these concepts in detail and understand how they interconnect to pose challenges to our digital security.

Threats

Threats refer to potential dangers or malicious activities that can exploit vulnerabilities and compromise the security of computer systems, networks, and data. Threats can be categorized into various types, including:

- **Malware**: Malicious software designed to damage, disrupt, or gain unauthorized access to computer systems. Examples include viruses, worms, Trojans, ransomware, and spyware.
- **Phishing**: Fraudulent attempts to obtain sensitive information by posing as a trustworthy entity in electronic communications, such as emails, messages, or websites.
- **Denial of Service (DoS) Attacks**: Attempts to overwhelm a system or network with excessive traffic, causing it to become slow, unresponsive, or unavailable to legitimate users.

Vulnerabilities

Vulnerabilities are weaknesses or flaws in computer systems, networks, or software that can be exploited by threats to gain unauthorized access, compromise data integrity, or disrupt operations. Common vulnerabilities include:

- **Software Bugs and Flaws**: Errors or oversights in software code that can be exploited to execute malicious actions or bypass security controls.

- **Outdated Software**: Running outdated or unsupported software can expose systems to known vulnerabilities that have been patched in newer versions.
- **Weak Passwords and Authentication**: Using weak passwords or failing to implement strong authentication measures can make it easier for attackers to gain unauthorized access to accounts and systems.

Attacks

An attack occurs when a threat exploits a vulnerability to compromise the security of a system, network, or data. Attacks can range from minor security breaches to major incidents that result in significant financial losses, reputational damage, and legal consequences. Some common attack methods include:

- **Exploitation of Software Vulnerabilities**: Attackers exploit known vulnerabilities in software to gain unauthorized access, execute malicious code, or steal sensitive information.
- **Social Engineering**: Manipulating individuals into divulging confidential information or performing actions that compromise security, often through deception and psychological manipulation.
- **Data Breaches**: Unauthorized access to and theft of sensitive data, such as personal information, financial records, and intellectual property, which can be used for identity theft, fraud, and other malicious activities.

Threats, vulnerabilities, and attacks form the intricate web of cybersecurity risks that organizations and individuals face in the digital landscape. Understanding these concepts and their interrelationships is crucial for developing effective cybersecurity strategies, implementing appropriate security measures, and responding promptly to security incidents.

By identifying potential threats, assessing vulnerabilities, and understanding attack methods, we can proactively manage risks, strengthen our defenses, and safeguard our digital assets against cyber threats.

In the following chapters, we will delve deeper into the various types of threats, vulnerabilities, and attack methods, exploring the techniques, tools, and best practices for mitigating risks and enhancing cybersecurity resilience.

So, let's continue our journey into the dynamic world of cybersecurity and equip ourselves with the knowledge and skills to protect our digital lives effectively!

2.3 Principles of Information Security

Information security is a complex and multifaceted discipline that aims to protect the confidentiality, integrity, and availability of information assets. To achieve robust and effective information security, several foundational principles guide the development, implementation, and maintenance of security controls and practices. In this section, we'll explore these fundamental principles and understand their significance in building a resilient information security framework.

Confidentiality

Confidentiality ensures that sensitive information is accessible only to authorized individuals or systems. Protecting confidentiality involves implementing measures such as:

- **Encryption**: Transforming data into an unreadable format using cryptographic algorithms to prevent unauthorized access.
- **Access Control**: Restricting access to information based on user roles, permissions, and authentication credentials.

Integrity

Integrity ensures that data remains accurate, consistent, and unaltered during storage, transmission, and processing. Maintaining data integrity involves:

- **Data Validation**: Implementing checks and controls to ensure data is accurate, complete, and free from errors.
- **Checksums and Digital Signatures**: Using checksums to verify data integrity and digital signatures to authenticate the source and integrity of data.

Availability

Availability ensures that information and resources are accessible and usable when needed. Ensuring availability involves:

- **Redundancy and Failover**: Implementing backup systems, redundant components, and failover mechanisms to minimize downtime and ensure continuous access to critical resources.
- **Disaster Recovery and Business Continuity Planning**: Developing and implementing plans and procedures to recover from system failures, disasters, or security incidents and maintain business operations.

Authenticity and Non-repudiation

- **Authenticity**: Verifying the identity of users, systems, and data to prevent unauthorized access and impersonation attacks.
- **Non-repudiation**: Ensuring that the origin and integrity of messages or transactions can be verified, preventing individuals from denying their actions or transactions.

Accountability

Accountability involves tracking and monitoring user activities, enforcing policies, and holding individuals accountable for their actions and behaviors. Implementing accountability measures helps deter malicious activities and ensure compliance with security policies and regulations.

Least Privilege

The principle of least privilege requires granting users the minimum levels of access necessary to perform their job functions. By restricting unnecessary access rights and privileges, organizations can minimize the risk of accidental or intentional misuse of information and resources.

Defense in Depth

Defense in depth is a layered approach to security that employs multiple security controls, measures, and strategies across various levels of an organization's infrastructure, applications, and data. By combining preventive, detective, and corrective controls, defense in depth enhances the overall security posture and resilience against evolving cyber threats.

The principles of information security serve as the cornerstone of a comprehensive and effective cybersecurity strategy. By adhering to these principles and integrating them into security policies, procedures, and practices, organizations can create a robust security framework that protects against a wide range of threats and vulnerabilities.

As we continue to explore the realm of cybersecurity in the following chapters, we will delve deeper into the practical applications of these principles, examining real-world scenarios, case studies, and best practices to help you build and maintain a resilient information security program.

So, let's continue our exploration of the fascinating world of cybersecurity and arm ourselves with the knowledge and insights to safeguard our digital assets and navigate the complexities of the digital age securely!

Chapter 3: Hacking Methodologies

In the realm of cybersecurity, understanding hacking methodologies is crucial for both defenders and practitioners. By gaining insight into how hackers think, plan, and execute attacks, organizations can better prepare their defenses and develop effective countermeasures. This chapter delves into various hacking methodologies, exploring the techniques, tools, and strategies used by hackers to exploit vulnerabilities and compromise systems.

Introduction to Hacking

Hacking is the unauthorized access, manipulation, or exploitation of computer systems, networks, and data. While some hackers engage in ethical hacking to identify and mitigate security vulnerabilities (known as white-hat hackers), others exploit these vulnerabilities for malicious purposes (black-hat hackers).

Reconnaissance

The reconnaissance phase involves gathering information about the target system, network, or organization. Hackers use various techniques, such as:

- **Open Source Intelligence (OSINT)**: Gathering publicly available information from websites, social media, forums, and other sources.

- **Scanning and Enumeration**: Using tools like Nmap to identify open ports, services, and vulnerabilities on target systems.

Vulnerability Analysis

In this phase, hackers identify and analyze vulnerabilities in the target system or network. They may use automated vulnerability scanners and manual testing techniques to uncover weaknesses that can be exploited.

Exploitation

Exploitation involves taking advantage of identified vulnerabilities to gain unauthorized access or control over the target system. Hackers may use:

- **Exploit Frameworks**: Tools like Metasploit provide a collection of exploits for known vulnerabilities, making it easier to launch attacks.
- **Payloads**: Malicious payloads, such as Trojans, backdoors, and ransomware, are delivered to compromised systems to maintain access, steal data, or disrupt operations.

Post-exploitation

After gaining access to the target system, hackers may perform various activities to maintain access, escalate privileges, and achieve their objectives. These activities can include:

- **Privilege Escalation**: Exploiting additional vulnerabilities to gain higher-level privileges and access to restricted resources.
- **Data Exfiltration**: Stealing sensitive information from the target system, which can be used for blackmail, fraud, or other malicious activities.
- **Covering Tracks**: Erasing evidence of the attack, altering logs, and removing traces to avoid detection and attribution.

Types of Hackers

Understanding the motivations and intentions behind hacking can help categorize hackers into different types:

- **White-Hat Hackers**: Ethical hackers who use their skills to identify and fix security vulnerabilities, often employed by organizations to perform penetration testing and security assessments.
- **Black-Hat Hackers**: Malicious hackers who exploit vulnerabilities for personal gain, financial profit, or malicious intent.
- **Grey-Hat Hackers**: A blend of both ethical and malicious hacking practices, often motivated by curiosity, challenge, or personal agendas.

Hacking methodologies provide a structured approach to understanding the lifecycle of a cyber-attack, from reconnaissance and vulnerability analysis to exploitation and post-exploitation activities. By gaining insights into these methodologies, organizations can enhance their security posture, develop proactive defense strategies, and mitigate the risks associated with cyber threats.

In the following chapters, we will delve deeper into specific hacking techniques, tools, and countermeasures, exploring practical examples, case studies, and best practices to help you build and maintain a resilient cybersecurity defense.

So, let's continue our journey into the fascinating world of cybersecurity and equip ourselves with the knowledge, skills, and insights to defend against cyber threats effectively!

3.1 Steps in Ethical Hacking

Ethical hacking, also known as penetration testing or white-hat hacking, involves legally and ethically identifying and exploiting vulnerabilities in systems, networks, and applications to assess and improve their security posture. Ethical hackers use their skills and knowledge to simulate real-world cyber-attacks in a controlled environment, helping organizations identify weaknesses and develop effective countermeasures. In this section, we'll explore the steps involved in ethical hacking and understand the methodology followed by ethical hackers.

1. Planning and Preparation

The first step in ethical hacking is planning and preparation. This involves defining the scope of the penetration test, identifying the target systems, and obtaining proper authorization from the organization to conduct the test. Ethical hackers also gather information about the target environment, including system architecture, network topology, and potential points of entry.

2. Reconnaissance

Reconnaissance, or information gathering, is the process of collecting data about the target system, network, or organization. Ethical hackers use various techniques to gather information, such as:

- **Open Source Intelligence (OSINT)**: Collecting publicly available information from websites, social media, forums, and other online sources.
- **Network Scanning**: Identifying live hosts, open ports, and running services using tools like Nmap.

3. Vulnerability Analysis

In this phase, ethical hackers identify and analyze potential vulnerabilities in the target environment. They may use automated vulnerability scanners and manual testing techniques to uncover weaknesses in systems, applications, and network configurations.

4. Exploitation

Once vulnerabilities are identified, ethical hackers attempt to exploit them to gain unauthorized access or control over the target systems. This involves using exploit frameworks and malicious payloads to demonstrate the impact of the vulnerabilities and validate their severity.

5. Post-exploitation

After successfully exploiting vulnerabilities, ethical hackers may perform various post-exploitation activities to maintain access, escalate privileges, and achieve their objectives. These activities can include:

- **Privilege Escalation**: Exploiting additional vulnerabilities to gain higher-level privileges and access to restricted resources.
- **Data Exfiltration**: Demonstrating the ability to steal sensitive information from the target system.

6. Reporting and Documentation

The final step in ethical hacking is reporting and documentation. Ethical hackers compile their findings, including identified vulnerabilities, exploited weaknesses, and recommended remediation measures, into a comprehensive report. This report is then shared with the organization's stakeholders, including IT teams, management, and decision-makers, to guide remediation efforts and improve the overall security posture.

Ethical hacking is a systematic and structured approach to identifying and mitigating security vulnerabilities in systems, networks, and applications. By following a well-defined methodology, ethical hackers can simulate real-world cyber-attacks, assess the effectiveness of existing security controls, and help organizations strengthen their defenses against potential threats.

As we continue to explore the fascinating world of cybersecurity in the following chapters, we will delve deeper into the tools, techniques, and best practices used in ethical hacking, providing practical insights, examples, and case studies to help you build and maintain a robust cybersecurity defense.

So, let's continue our journey into the dynamic and challenging realm of ethical hacking, equipping ourselves with the knowledge, skills, and insights to protect and defend against cyber threats effectively!

3.2 Reconnaissance and Footprinting

Reconnaissance and footprinting are critical initial phases in the ethical hacking process. These phases involve gathering information about the target system, network, or organization to understand its structure, vulnerabilities, and potential points of entry. By collecting and analyzing this information, ethical hackers can identify potential weaknesses, plan their attack strategy, and simulate real-world cyber-attacks effectively. In this section, we'll delve into the concepts of reconnaissance and footprinting and explore the techniques used by ethical hackers in these phases.

What is Reconnaissance?

Reconnaissance, also known as information gathering or OSINT (Open Source Intelligence), is the initial phase of ethical hacking where hackers gather information about the target system, network, or organization. This information can include:

- **Domain Names**: Identifying domain names associated with the target organization, including primary domains, subdomains, and related domains.
- **IP Addresses**: Discovering IP addresses associated with the target systems and network infrastructure.
- **Employee Information**: Gathering information about employees, including names, email addresses, job titles, and contact details, from sources like corporate websites, social media, and professional networking sites.

Techniques for Reconnaissance

Ethical hackers use various techniques to gather information during the reconnaissance phase:

- **DNS Enumeration**: Using tools like nslookup, dig, or host to gather information about DNS records, including MX, CNAME, and TXT records.
- **Web Scraping**: Extracting information from websites using automated tools or scripts to collect data like email addresses, contact details, and organizational structure.
- **Social Engineering**: Gathering information through social engineering techniques, such as pretexting, phishing, and impersonation, to manipulate individuals into revealing confidential information.

What is Footprinting?

Footprinting involves gathering detailed information about the target system, network, or organization to create a complete profile or "footprint." This profile includes:

- **Network Topology**: Understanding the network architecture, including IP addresses, subnets, routers, switches, and firewalls.
- **System Architecture**: Identifying operating systems, software, services, and applications running on the target systems.
- **Security Measures**: Assessing the existing security controls, configurations, and policies to identify potential weaknesses and vulnerabilities.

Techniques for Footprinting

Ethical hackers use various techniques for footprinting:

- **Network Scanning**: Using tools like Nmap or Masscan to identify live hosts, open ports, and running services within the target network.
- **Banner Grabbing**: Collecting information about running services, software versions, and configurations by connecting to open ports using tools like Netcat or Telnet.
- **WHOIS Lookup**: Retrieving domain registration information, including domain owners, registration dates, and contact details, using WHOIS lookup tools.

Reconnaissance and footprinting are essential phases in the ethical hacking process, providing valuable insights into the target environment's structure, vulnerabilities, and potential points of entry. By systematically gathering and analyzing information, ethical hackers can develop a comprehensive understanding of the target system, network, or organization, enabling them to plan and execute effective penetration testing and vulnerability assessment activities.

As we continue to explore the fascinating world of cybersecurity in the following chapters, we will delve deeper into the tools, techniques, and best practices used in reconnaissance, footprinting, and other phases of ethical hacking, providing practical insights, examples, and case studies to help you build and maintain a robust cybersecurity defense.

So, let's continue our journey into the dynamic and challenging realm of ethical hacking, equipping ourselves with the knowledge, skills, and insights to protect and defend against cyber threats effectively!

3.3 Scanning and Enumeration

Scanning and enumeration are pivotal phases in the ethical hacking process, following reconnaissance and footprinting. These phases involve actively probing the target system, network, or application to identify live hosts, open ports, running services, and potential vulnerabilities. By conducting thorough scanning and enumeration, ethical hackers can validate the information gathered during the reconnaissance phase and pinpoint specific areas for exploitation. In this section, we'll delve into the concepts of scanning and enumeration and explore the techniques used by ethical hackers in these phases.

What is Scanning?

Scanning is the process of actively probing the target system or network to discover live hosts, open ports, and running services. Ethical hackers use various scanning techniques to gather detailed information about the target environment, including:

- **Port Scanning**: Identifying open ports on target hosts using tools like Nmap, Masscan, or Netcat to determine available services and potential points of entry.
- **Network Scanning**: Mapping the network topology and identifying live hosts, routers, switches, and firewalls to understand the target's infrastructure.
- **Vulnerability Scanning**: Using automated vulnerability scanners like OpenVAS or Nessus to identify known vulnerabilities in the target systems and applications.

Techniques for Scanning

Ethical hackers employ several techniques for scanning:

- **TCP Connect Scanning**: Establishing a full TCP connection with target hosts to determine the state of open ports and services.
- **SYN Stealth Scanning**: Sending SYN packets to target hosts and analyzing responses to identify open ports without completing the TCP handshake.
- **UDP Scanning**: Probing target hosts for open UDP ports and services, which do not require a connection handshake like TCP.

What is Enumeration?

Enumeration is the process of extracting additional information about the target system, network, or application by interacting with discovered services and systems. This phase aims to identify users, shares, resources, and other valuable data that can be leveraged for further exploitation. Techniques used in enumeration include:

- **Service Enumeration**: Identifying services running on open ports, including version details, configurations, and potential vulnerabilities.
- **User Enumeration**: Gathering information about users, groups, and accounts on target systems using techniques like brute-force attacks, user enumeration scripts, or LDAP queries.
- **Network Enumeration**: Mapping network shares, identifying network resources, and discovering network protocols and configurations to understand the target's infrastructure and potential attack vectors.

Techniques for Enumeration

Ethical hackers use various techniques for enumeration:

- **Banner Grabbing**: Collecting information about running services, software versions, and configurations by connecting to open ports using tools like Netcat or Telnet.

- **LDAP Enumeration**: Querying Lightweight Directory Access Protocol (LDAP) servers to retrieve information about users, groups, and organizational structures.
- **SNMP Enumeration**: Extracting information from Simple Network Management Protocol (SNMP) enabled devices to gather data about network devices, configurations, and performance metrics.

Scanning and enumeration are crucial phases in the ethical hacking process, enabling ethical hackers to gather detailed information about the target system, network, or application and identify potential vulnerabilities and attack vectors. By employing a combination of scanning and enumeration techniques, ethical hackers can validate their initial findings, uncover hidden weaknesses, and develop a comprehensive understanding of the target environment's security posture.

As we continue to explore the fascinating world of cybersecurity in the following chapters, we will delve deeper into the tools, techniques, and best practices used in scanning, enumeration, and other phases of ethical hacking, providing practical insights, examples, and case studies to help you build and maintain a robust cybersecurity defense.

So, let's continue our journey into the dynamic and challenging realm of ethical hacking, equipping ourselves with the knowledge, skills, and insights to protect and defend against cyber threats effectively!

3.4 Gaining Access

Gaining access is a critical phase in the ethical hacking process, following reconnaissance, footprinting, scanning, and enumeration. In this phase, ethical hackers attempt to exploit identified vulnerabilities to gain unauthorized access or control over the target system, network, or application. By successfully gaining access, ethical hackers validate the effectiveness of identified vulnerabilities and demonstrate the potential impact of security weaknesses. In this section, we'll delve into the concepts of gaining access and explore the techniques used by ethical hackers in this phase.

Exploitation Techniques

Ethical hackers use various exploitation techniques to gain access to target systems:

- **Buffer Overflow**: Exploiting buffer overflow vulnerabilities to overwrite memory and execute arbitrary code on the target system.
- **SQL Injection**: Injecting malicious SQL queries into web applications to manipulate databases and gain unauthorized access to data.
- **Cross-Site Scripting (XSS)**: Injecting malicious scripts into web pages to steal cookies, hijack sessions, or deface websites.
- **Command Injection**: Exploiting command injection vulnerabilities in applications to execute arbitrary commands on the underlying system.

Post-Exploitation Activities

After gaining initial access, ethical hackers may perform various post-exploitation activities to maintain control, escalate privileges, and achieve their objectives:

- **Privilege Escalation**: Exploiting additional vulnerabilities to gain higher-level privileges and access to restricted resources.
- **Persistence**: Establishing persistent access to the target system by creating backdoors, scheduled tasks, or hidden processes.
- **Data Exfiltration**: Transferring sensitive data from the target system to an external location using methods like file transfers, email, or remote access tools.

Tools and Frameworks

Ethical hackers leverage various tools and frameworks to facilitate the exploitation and post-exploitation phases:

- **Metasploit Framework**: A powerful exploitation framework that provides a collection of exploits, payloads, and post-exploitation modules to aid in penetration testing and vulnerability assessment.
- **Exploit Databases**: Online repositories like Exploit Database, Packet Storm, and GitHub provide a wealth of exploits for known vulnerabilities.
- **Custom Scripts and Tools**: Developing custom scripts and tools tailored to specific vulnerabilities or target environments to exploit and control target systems effectively.

Gaining access is a crucial phase in the ethical hacking process, enabling ethical hackers to validate the effectiveness of identified vulnerabilities and demonstrate the potential impact of security weaknesses. By leveraging various exploitation techniques, tools, and frameworks, ethical hackers can simulate real-world cyber-attacks, assess the security posture of target systems, and provide actionable insights and recommendations for remediation.

As we continue to explore the fascinating world of cybersecurity in the following chapters, we will delve deeper into the tools, techniques, and best practices used in gaining access, post-exploitation activities, and other phases of ethical hacking, providing practical insights, examples, and case studies to help you build and maintain a robust cybersecurity defense.

3.5 Maintaining Access

Maintaining access is a crucial phase in the ethical hacking process that follows gaining access and post-exploitation activities. In this phase, ethical hackers aim to retain persistent control over the compromised system, network, or application to continue unauthorized access, gather more information, or execute further malicious activities. By maintaining access, ethical hackers can demonstrate the long-term impact of security vulnerabilities and provide organizations with insights into potential risks and vulnerabilities that require attention. In this section, we'll delve into the concepts of maintaining access and explore the techniques used by ethical hackers in this phase.

Techniques for Maintaining Access

Ethical hackers use various techniques to maintain persistent access to the compromised systems:

- **Backdoors**: Creating hidden entry points or backdoors in the target system to allow unauthorized access in the future without detection.
- **Rootkits**: Installing rootkits to conceal malicious activities, processes, and files, makes it difficult for administrators to detect and remove unauthorized access.
- **Scheduled Tasks**: Setting up scheduled tasks or cron jobs to execute malicious payloads at specified intervals or under specific conditions.
- **Remote Access Tools**: Installing remote access tools like Remote Access Trojans (RATs) or Remote Administration Tools (RATs) to control compromised systems remotely.

Tools and Frameworks

Ethical hackers leverage various tools and frameworks to facilitate the maintaining access phase:

- **Netcat**: A versatile networking tool that can be used to create backdoors, establish reverse shells, and transfer files between systems.
- **Meterpreter**: A post-exploitation payload used with the Metasploit Framework that provides a range of features to

maintain access, escalate privileges, and execute commands on compromised systems.

- **Custom Scripts and Tools**: Developing custom scripts and tools tailored to specific vulnerabilities or target environments to maintain persistent access and control target systems effectively.

Evading Detection

Maintaining access often involves evading detection and remaining undetected by security tools, monitoring solutions, and administrators:

- **Stealth Techniques**: Employing stealth techniques like obfuscation, encryption, and steganography to hide malicious activities and evade detection.
- **Anti-Virus Evasion**: Using techniques to bypass or disable antivirus solutions, intrusion detection/prevention systems (IDS/IPS), and other security mechanisms.
- **Monitoring and Cleaning**: Continuously monitoring the compromised systems for signs of detection and cleaning logs, traces, and other evidence to maintain stealth and anonymity.

Maintaining access is a critical phase in the ethical hacking process, enabling ethical hackers to demonstrate the long-term impact of security vulnerabilities and provide organizations with insights into potential risks and vulnerabilities that require attention. By leveraging various techniques, tools, and frameworks, ethical hackers can maintain persistent control over compromised systems, evade detection, and simulate real-world cyber-attacks to assess the security posture of target environments effectively.

As we continue to explore the fascinating world of cybersecurity in the following chapters, we will delve deeper into the tools, techniques, and best practices used in maintaining access, evading detection, and other advanced phases of ethical hacking, providing practical insights, examples, and case studies to help you build and maintain a robust cybersecurity defense.

3.6 Clearing Tracks

Clearing tracks is a pivotal phase in the ethical hacking process that follows maintaining access. In this phase, ethical hackers aim to remove any evidence of their presence and activities from the compromised system, network, or application to evade detection, maintain anonymity, and cover their tracks effectively. By clearing tracks, ethical hackers can simulate the actions of malicious actors and demonstrate the importance of monitoring and detection capabilities in cybersecurity defense strategies. In this section, we'll delve into the concepts of clearing tracks and explore the techniques used by ethical hackers in this phase.

Importance of Clearing Tracks

Clearing tracks is essential for ethical hackers to maintain stealth, evade detection, and preserve the integrity of the testing environment. By removing traces of their activities, ethical hackers can simulate the actions of real-world attackers and help organizations understand the challenges involved in detecting and responding to cyber threats effectively.

Techniques for Clearing Tracks

Ethical hackers use various techniques to clear tracks and remove evidence of their activities:

- **Log Cleaning**: Deleting or modifying system logs, event logs, and application logs to remove records of unauthorized access, commands executed, and other suspicious activities.
- **File Deletion**: Removing temporary files, script files, malicious payloads, and other artifacts left behind during the exploitation and post-exploitation phases.
- **Registry Cleaning**: Modifying or deleting registry entries, configuration settings, and startup items associated with malicious activities and persistent access methods.
- **Network Cleaning**: Closing active connections, terminating remote sessions, and removing network traces and artifacts to erase evidence of remote access and data exfiltration.

Tools and Frameworks

Ethical hackers leverage various tools and frameworks to facilitate the clearing tracks phase:

- **Sdelete**: A command-line utility that securely deletes files and cleans free disk space to prevent recovery and remove traces of deleted files.

- **CCleaner**: A popular system optimization and cleaning tool that can be used to remove temporary files, browser history, cookies, and other potentially sensitive information.
- **Custom Scripts and Tools**: Developing custom scripts and tools tailored to specific environments and requirements to automate the process of clearing tracks and removing evidence effectively.

Best Practices for Clearing Tracks

Ethical hackers follow best practices to ensure thorough and effective clearing of tracks:

- **Documentation**: Maintaining detailed documentation of activities, commands executed, and changes made during the testing process to track and verify the clearing tracks activities.
- **Verification**: Performing thorough verification and validation checks to ensure that all traces of activities and artifacts have been removed successfully.
- **Compliance and Ethics**: Adhering to ethical guidelines, legal requirements, and compliance standards to ensure responsible and lawful conduct during the testing process.

Clearing tracks is a critical phase in the ethical hacking process, enabling ethical hackers to maintain stealth, evade detection, and cover their tracks effectively. By employing various techniques, tools, and best practices, ethical hackers can simulate the actions of real-world attackers and provide organizations with valuable insights into the challenges involved in detecting and responding to cyber threats effectively.

As we continue to explore the fascinating world of cybersecurity in the following chapters, we will delve deeper into the tools, techniques, and best practices used in clearing tracks, maintaining anonymity, and other advanced phases of ethical hacking, providing practical insights, examples, and case studies to help you build and maintain a robust cybersecurity defense.

Chapter 4: Hacking Tools and Techniques

In the ever-evolving landscape of cybersecurity, hackers continuously develop sophisticated tools and techniques to exploit vulnerabilities and compromise systems. Understanding these tools and techniques is essential for both cybersecurity professionals defending against cyber threats and ethical hackers conducting penetration testing and vulnerability assessments. This chapter explores a range of hacking tools and techniques used by hackers and ethical hackers alike, providing insights into their functionalities, applications, and best practices for their use.

1. Introduction to Hacking Tools

Hacking tools are software applications designed to assist hackers in identifying vulnerabilities, exploiting weaknesses, and gaining unauthorized access to systems, networks, and applications. These tools range from simple utilities for network scanning and password cracking to advanced frameworks for exploitation and post-exploitation activities. In this section, we'll introduce you to some of the most commonly used hacking tools and their functionalities.

Common Hacking Tools

- **Nmap**: A powerful network scanning tool used for host discovery, port scanning, service enumeration, and vulnerability scanning.
- **Metasploit Framework**: An advanced exploitation framework that provides a collection of exploits, payloads, and post-

exploitation modules for penetration testing and vulnerability assessment.

- **Wireshark**: A widely-used network protocol analyzer that captures and analyzes network traffic in real time to identify suspicious activities, protocols, and data packets.
- **John the Ripper**: A fast password cracker that can be used to audit password strength, crack encrypted passwords, and perform brute-force attacks.
- **Hydra**: A parallelized login cracker that supports various protocols, including HTTP, FTP, SSH, and SMB, enabling hackers to perform brute-force attacks on login credentials.

2. Common Hacking Techniques

Hacking techniques encompass a wide range of methods and strategies employed by hackers to exploit vulnerabilities and compromise systems. These techniques can be categorized into various types, including network exploitation, web application attacks, social engineering, and malware deployment. In this section, we'll explore some of the most prevalent hacking techniques and their applications.

Common Hacking Techniques

- **Phishing Attacks**: Deceptive techniques used to trick users into disclosing sensitive information, such as usernames, passwords, and credit card details, usually through emails, websites, or messages.

- **SQL Injection**: Exploiting vulnerabilities in web applications to manipulate SQL queries and gain unauthorized access to databases, extract sensitive data, or execute arbitrary commands.
- **Man-in-the-Middle (MitM) Attacks**: Intercepting and relaying communication between two parties without their knowledge, enabling hackers to eavesdrop, modify, or manipulate data transmitted over the network.
- **Cross-Site Scripting (XSS)**: Injecting malicious scripts into web pages viewed by users to steal cookies, hijack sessions, or deface websites.
- **Denial of Service (DoS) and Distributed Denial of Service (DDoS) Attacks**: Overwhelming target systems or networks with excessive traffic or requests, causing them to become slow, unresponsive, or unavailable to legitimate users.

3. Ethical Hacking and Penetration Testing

Ethical hacking and penetration testing involve simulating real-world cyber-attacks on systems, networks, and applications to identify vulnerabilities, assess security controls, and recommend remediation measures. Ethical hackers use a combination of hacking tools and techniques to perform controlled, authorized tests and help organizations strengthen their cybersecurity defenses. In this section, we'll discuss the importance of ethical hacking and penetration testing, as well as the methodologies employed in these practices.

Ethical Hacking Methodology

- **Reconnaissance**: Gathering information about the target system, network, or organization through open-source intelligence (OSINT), scanning, and enumeration techniques.
- **Scanning and Enumeration**: Identifying live hosts, open ports, and running services to uncover potential vulnerabilities and attack vectors.
- **Gaining Access**: Exploiting identified vulnerabilities to gain unauthorized access or control over the target environment.
- **Maintaining Access**: Establishing persistent control over compromised systems to simulate advanced persistent threats (APTs) and demonstrate the long-term impact of security weaknesses.
- **Clearing Tracks**: Removing evidence of activities and maintaining stealth to simulate the actions of real-world attackers and assess detection and response capabilities.

Hacking tools and techniques play a pivotal role in the cybersecurity landscape, shaping the strategies and tactics employed by both malicious hackers and ethical hackers. By understanding these tools and techniques, cybersecurity professionals can better defend against cyber threats, while ethical hackers can conduct effective penetration testing and vulnerability assessments to help organizations strengthen their security posture.

As we continue to explore the fascinating world of cybersecurity in the following chapters, we will delve deeper into specific hacking tools, techniques, and best practices, providing practical insights, examples, and case studies to help you build and maintain a robust cybersecurity defense.

4.1 Introduction to Hacking Tools

Hacking tools are specialized software applications designed to assist hackers, cybersecurity professionals, and ethical hackers in identifying vulnerabilities, exploiting weaknesses, and gaining unauthorized access to systems, networks, and applications. These tools range from simple utilities for network scanning and password cracking to advanced frameworks for exploitation and post-exploitation activities. In this section, we'll introduce you to some of the most commonly used hacking tools, exploring their functionalities, applications, and relevance in the cybersecurity landscape.

Nmap

Nmap (Network Mapper) is a versatile and powerful network scanning tool widely used by hackers and cybersecurity professionals for host discovery, port scanning, service enumeration, and vulnerability scanning. Nmap can scan large networks, providing valuable insights into the network topology, active hosts, open ports, and running services. It supports various scanning techniques, including TCP connect scanning, SYN stealth scanning, and UDP scanning, allowing users to customize their scans based on specific requirements and objectives.

Metasploit Framework

Metasploit Framework is an advanced exploitation framework that provides a comprehensive collection of exploits, payloads, and post-exploitation modules for penetration testing, vulnerability assessment, and ethical hacking. Developed by Rapid7, Metasploit simplifies the process of identifying and exploiting vulnerabilities in target systems, enabling ethical hackers to simulate real-world cyber-attacks effectively. It features a user-friendly interface, extensive exploit database, and integration with other tools, making it a preferred choice for both novice and experienced ethical hackers.

Wireshark

Wireshark is a popular network protocol analyzer that captures and analyzes network traffic in real time to identify suspicious activities, protocols, and data packets. Formerly known as Ethereal, Wireshark offers a rich set of features for deep packet inspection, protocol decoding, and network troubleshooting. It supports various network protocols, including TCP/IP, UDP, ICMP, and HTTP, allowing users to dissect network traffic, filter packets, and analyze communication patterns to detect anomalies and potential security threats.

John the Ripper

John the Ripper is a fast and efficient password cracker used by hackers and cybersecurity professionals to audit password strength, crack encrypted passwords, and perform brute-force attacks. It supports various password hash formats and encryption algorithms, including DES, MD5, SHA-1, and bcrypt, making it a versatile tool for password auditing and recovery. John the Ripper can run on multiple platforms and offers a command-line interface with flexible options and configurations, enabling users to customize their cracking sessions based on specific requirements and constraints.

Hydra

Hydra is a parallelized login cracker that supports various protocols and services, including HTTP, FTP, SSH, and SMB. Developed by THC (The Hacker's Choice), Hydra enables hackers to perform brute-force attacks on login credentials, exploiting weak passwords and authentication mechanisms to gain unauthorized access to target systems. It features a user-friendly interface, multi-threaded operation, and extensive protocol support, making it a powerful tool for password-guessing and credential-stuffing attacks.

Hacking tools are essential components in the cybersecurity arsenal, providing hackers, cybersecurity professionals, and ethical hackers with the capabilities to identify vulnerabilities, exploit weaknesses, and assess security controls effectively. By leveraging these tools, individuals can simulate real-world cyber-attacks, test the resilience of their defenses, and develop robust cybersecurity strategies to protect against evolving cyber threats.

As we delve deeper into the fascinating world of cybersecurity in the following sections, we will explore these hacking tools and others in greater detail, providing practical insights, examples, and case studies to help you understand their functionalities, applications, and best practices for their use.

4.3 Password Cracking Tools

Password cracking is a critical component of cybersecurity assessments, enabling cybersecurity professionals and ethical hackers to audit password strength, recover lost passwords, and identify weak authentication mechanisms. Password cracking tools leverage various techniques, including brute-force attacks, dictionary attacks, and rainbow table attacks, to decrypt encrypted passwords and gain unauthorized access to user accounts. In this section, we'll explore some of the most popular and effective password-cracking tools, discussing their features, functionalities, and best practices for their use.

John the Ripper

John the Ripper is a fast and efficient password cracker widely used by hackers, cybersecurity professionals, and ethical hackers to audit password strength, crack encrypted passwords, and perform brute-force attacks. It supports various password hash formats and encryption algorithms, including DES, MD5, SHA-1, and bcrypt, making it a versatile tool for password auditing and recovery. John the Ripper can run on multiple platforms and offers a command-line interface with flexible options and configurations, enabling users to customize their cracking sessions based on specific requirements and constraints.

Hashcat

Hashcat is an advanced password recovery tool that supports the cracking of a wide range of hash algorithms, including MD5, SHA-1, SHA-256, and bcrypt. Developed by Jens "Atom" Steube, Hashcat leverages the power of GPU acceleration to deliver lightning-fast password-cracking performance, making it one of the most potent tools in the password-cracking arsenal. It supports multiple attack modes, including brute-force, dictionary, and mask attacks, and offers robust rule-based attack customization capabilities for optimizing cracking sessions and maximizing success rates.

Hydra

Hydra is a parallelized login cracker that supports various protocols and services, including HTTP, FTP, SSH, and SMB. Developed by THC (The Hacker's Choice), Hydra enables hackers to perform brute-force attacks on login credentials, exploiting weak passwords and authentication mechanisms to gain unauthorized access to target systems. It features a user-friendly interface, multi-threaded operation, and extensive protocol support, making it a powerful tool for password-guessing and credential-stuffing attacks.

Cain & Abel

Cain & Abel is a comprehensive password recovery tool that offers a wide range of features for auditing and recovering passwords from various sources, including Windows SAM databases, wireless networks, and encrypted files. Developed by Massimiliano Montoro, Cain & Abel supports multiple attack methods, including dictionary, brute-force, and rainbow table attacks, and provides advanced sniffing and cracking capabilities for network protocols such as HTTP, FTP, and SMTP. It features a user-friendly interface with graphical tools for analyzing captured data, decrypting encrypted passwords, and recovering lost credentials.

Password cracking tools are indispensable assets in the cybersecurity toolkit, providing valuable capabilities for auditing password strength, recovering lost passwords, and identifying weak authentication mechanisms. By leveraging these tools, cybersecurity professionals can assess the resilience of their password policies, educate users on password best practices, and simulate real-world password attacks to strengthen their security defenses.

As we continue to explore the fascinating world of cybersecurity in the following sections, we will delve deeper into the capabilities, features, and best practices associated with these password-cracking tools, providing practical insights, examples, and case studies to help you master the art of password auditing and recovery.

4.4 Vulnerability Assessment Tools

Vulnerability assessment is a critical process in cybersecurity that involves identifying, quantifying, and prioritizing vulnerabilities in systems, networks, and applications. Vulnerability assessment tools play a pivotal role in this process, enabling cybersecurity professionals, ethical hackers, and organizations to detect and analyze security weaknesses, assess the potential impact of vulnerabilities, and develop effective remediation strategies. In this section, we'll explore some of the most popular and effective vulnerability assessment tools, discussing their features, functionalities, and best practices for their use.

OpenVAS (Open Vulnerability Assessment System)

OpenVAS is a comprehensive vulnerability scanning and management tool that offers a wide range of features for detecting, assessing, and managing security vulnerabilities in systems and networks. It includes a powerful scanning engine, extensive vulnerability database, and user-friendly web-based interface, making it a preferred choice for organizations and cybersecurity professionals conducting vulnerability assessments. OpenVAS supports various scanning profiles, including full scans, fast scans, and targeted scans, and provides detailed reports with actionable insights and remediation recommendations.

Nessus

Nessus is a widely-used vulnerability scanning tool developed by Tenable Network Security, offering advanced capabilities for identifying, assessing, and prioritizing vulnerabilities across a wide range of environments, including on-premises, cloud, and hybrid infrastructures. Nessus features a robust scanning engine, comprehensive vulnerability database, and customizable reporting capabilities, making it a versatile tool for vulnerability management and compliance monitoring. It supports various scanning options, including credentialed scans, non-credentialed scans, and compliance scans, and offers integration with other security tools and platforms for streamlined vulnerability assessment workflows.

Retina

Retina is a vulnerability management solution developed by BeyondTrust, designed to help organizations identify, prioritize, and remediate security vulnerabilities across their IT infrastructure. Retina offers a comprehensive suite of features, including vulnerability scanning, configuration assessment, and compliance reporting, enabling organizations to maintain a strong security posture and meet regulatory requirements. It supports automated scanning, scheduled assessments, and real-time monitoring, providing organizations with continuous visibility into their security vulnerabilities and risks.

QualysGuard

QualysGuard is a cloud-based vulnerability management platform that offers a range of automated solutions for vulnerability scanning, assessment, and remediation. Developed by Qualys, Inc., QualysGuard provides a scalable and flexible approach to vulnerability management, allowing organizations to streamline their security operations, reduce complexity, and improve efficiency. It features a centralized dashboard, customizable reporting, and integration with other security tools and platforms, making it an ideal choice for organizations looking to enhance their vulnerability assessment capabilities and strengthen their security defenses.

Vulnerability assessment tools are essential components in the cybersecurity toolkit, providing valuable capabilities for identifying, assessing, and managing security vulnerabilities across systems, networks, and applications. By leveraging these tools, organizations and cybersecurity professionals can gain insights into their security posture, prioritize remediation efforts, and develop effective strategies to mitigate risks and protect against cyber threats.

As we continue to explore the fascinating world of cybersecurity in the following sections, we will delve deeper into the capabilities, features, and best practices associated with these vulnerability assessment tools, providing practical insights, examples, and case studies to help you master the art of vulnerability management and remediation.

4.5 Exploitation Tools

Exploitation tools are specialized software applications and frameworks designed to identify, exploit, and leverage vulnerabilities in systems, networks, and applications. These tools are instrumental for cybersecurity professionals, ethical hackers, and penetration testers in demonstrating the real-world impact of security vulnerabilities and assessing the resilience of target environments against cyber-attacks. In this section, we'll explore some of the most powerful and widely used exploitation tools, discussing their features, functionalities, and best practices for their use.

Metasploit Framework

Metasploit Framework is an advanced exploitation framework that provides a comprehensive collection of exploits, payloads, and post-exploitation modules for penetration testing, vulnerability assessment, and ethical hacking. Developed by Rapid7, Metasploit simplifies the process of identifying and exploiting vulnerabilities in target systems, enabling ethical hackers to simulate real-world cyber-attacks effectively. It features a user-friendly interface, extensive exploit database, and integration with other tools, making it a preferred choice for both novice and experienced penetration testers.

Cobalt Strike

Cobalt Strike is a powerful penetration testing platform that offers a range of tools and features for exploiting vulnerabilities, conducting red teaming exercises, and simulating advanced cyber-attacks. Developed by Strategic Cyber LLC, Cobalt Strike provides a robust environment for penetration testers to emulate threat actor tactics, techniques, and procedures (TTPs), facilitating realistic and impactful security assessments. It features a multi-tabbed interface, built-in team collaboration capabilities, and comprehensive post-exploitation modules, making it a versatile tool for advanced penetration testing and adversarial simulation.

Exploit Frameworks (ExploitDB, CVE Details)

Exploit Database (ExploitDB) and CVE Details are online repositories that provide a wealth of exploits, vulnerabilities, and security advisories for various systems, applications, and devices. These platforms enable cybersecurity professionals and ethical hackers to access and leverage a vast collection of exploits and vulnerability information, facilitating the identification and exploitation of security weaknesses in target environments. ExploitDB features a search-friendly interface, detailed exploit descriptions, and download links for exploit code, while CVE Details offers comprehensive vulnerability statistics, severity ratings, and links to related security resources.

BeEF (Browser Exploitation Framework)

BeEF (Browser Exploitation Framework) is a powerful exploitation tool designed to target web browsers and leverage client-side vulnerabilities to gain unauthorized access to user systems. Developed by Wade Alcorn and maintained by a vibrant community, BeEF enables penetration testers to demonstrate the risks associated with browser-based attacks, phishing, and client-side exploitation. It features a web-based user interface, extensive browser command modules, and integration capabilities with other tools, making it an invaluable asset for assessing and mitigating web application security risks.

Exploitation tools are essential assets in the cybersecurity toolkit, providing valuable capabilities for identifying, exploiting, and leveraging vulnerabilities in target systems, networks, and applications. By leveraging these tools, cybersecurity professionals and ethical hackers can simulate real-world cyber-attacks, assess the impact of security vulnerabilities, and develop effective strategies to mitigate risks and strengthen security defenses.

As we continue to explore the fascinating world of cybersecurity in the following sections, we will delve deeper into the capabilities, features, and best practices associated with these exploitation tools, providing practical insights, examples, and case studies to help you master the art of ethical hacking, penetration testing, and vulnerability exploitation.

Chapter 5: Wireless Network Security

In today's interconnected world, wireless networks have become an integral part of our daily lives, enabling seamless communication, collaboration, and access to information anytime, anywhere. However, the convenience offered by wireless technology also introduces security risks and vulnerabilities that can be exploited by cybercriminals to compromise sensitive data, intercept communications, and gain unauthorized access to network resources. In this chapter, we'll explore the fundamentals of wireless network security, discussing the challenges, threats, and best practices for securing wireless networks effectively.

1. Understanding Wireless Networks

Wireless networks, often referred to as Wi-Fi networks, use radio waves to transmit data between devices without the need for physical wired connections. These networks are commonly deployed in homes, businesses, public spaces, and mobile devices, providing users with flexible and convenient access to the internet and network resources. Wireless networks can be categorized into several types, including:

- **Wi-Fi (Wireless Fidelity)**: The most popular type of wireless network, commonly used in homes, offices, and public hotspots to provide internet access to users.
- **Bluetooth**: A short-range wireless technology used for connecting devices such as smartphones, tablets, and wearable devices to other networks.

- **NFC (Near Field Communication)**: A contactless communication technology used for secure data exchange between devices nearby, commonly found in mobile payment systems and access control solutions.

2. Wireless Security Threats and Vulnerabilities

Wireless networks are susceptible to various security threats and vulnerabilities that can compromise the confidentiality, integrity, and availability of sensitive information and network resources. Some of the common wireless security threats include:

- **Eavesdropping**: Unauthorized interception of wireless communications to capture sensitive data, such as passwords, credit card numbers, and personal information.
- **Man-in-the-Middle (MitM) Attacks**: Interception and modification of wireless communications between two parties to eavesdrop, manipulate, or impersonate legitimate users.
- **Rogue Access Points**: Unauthorized wireless access points deployed by attackers to lure unsuspecting users and capture sensitive information or launch attacks on connected devices.
- **Denial of Service (DoS) Attacks**: Overloading wireless networks with excessive traffic or malicious requests to disrupt service availability and degrade network performance.

3. Best Practices for Wireless Network Security

Securing wireless networks requires a multi-layered approach that addresses various aspects of network design, configuration, monitoring, and management. Here are some best practices for enhancing wireless network security:

- **Enable Encryption**: Use strong encryption protocols such as WPA3 (Wi-Fi Protected Access 3) to encrypt wireless communications and protect sensitive data from unauthorized access and interception.
- **Change Default Settings**: Modify default SSIDs (Service Set Identifiers), passwords, and administrative credentials to prevent unauthorized access and reduce the risk of exploitation.
- **Implement Network Segmentation**: Separate wireless networks from critical network resources using VLANs (Virtual Local Area Networks) and firewall rules to contain potential threats and limit the scope of attacks.
- **Enable Network Monitoring and Logging**: Deploy intrusion detection and prevention systems (IDS/IPS) and enable logging and monitoring capabilities to detect suspicious activities, identify security incidents, and facilitate timely response and remediation.
- **Update and Patch Regularly**: Keep wireless routers, access points, and devices up to date with the latest firmware and security patches to address known vulnerabilities and protect against emerging threats.

Wireless network security is a critical aspect of cybersecurity that requires careful planning, implementation, and management to protect against evolving threats and vulnerabilities. By understanding the fundamentals of wireless networks, identifying common security threats, and adopting best practices for wireless network security, organizations, and individuals can create a secure and resilient wireless environment that enables safe and productive connectivity.

As we continue to explore the fascinating world of cybersecurity in the following chapters, we will delve deeper into the intricacies of wireless network security, exploring advanced techniques, tools, and strategies for securing wireless networks effectively and mitigating the risks associated with wireless technology.

5.1 Basics of Wireless Networks

Wireless networks have revolutionized the way we connect, communicate, and collaborate in both personal and professional settings. Understanding the basics of wireless networks is essential for grasping their functionality, components, and operation principles, which are crucial for effective wireless network security management. In this section, we'll delve into the fundamentals of wireless networks, exploring their types, components, and key concepts that underpin their operation.

Types of Wireless Networks

Wireless networks can be categorized into several types based on their coverage area, technology, and application. Some of the common types of wireless networks include:

- **Wireless Local Area Network (WLAN)**: WLANs, commonly known as Wi-Fi networks, are designed to provide wireless connectivity within a limited geographical area, such as homes, offices, and public hotspots. They use radio frequency (RF) signals to transmit data between devices, allowing users to access the internet and network resources without physical wired connections.
- **Wireless Personal Area Network (WPAN)**: WPANs are short-range wireless networks that connect devices within close proximity, typically within a few meters. Bluetooth and NFC (Near Field Communication) are examples of WPAN technologies commonly used for connecting smartphones, tablets, wearable devices, and other peripherals.
- **Wireless Metropolitan Area Network (WMAN)**: WMANs, also known as WiMAX networks, are designed to provide wireless connectivity over a broader geographical area, such as a city or a campus. They use long-range wireless transmission technologies to deliver high-speed internet access to users in urban and suburban areas.
- **Wireless Wide Area Network (WWAN)**: WWANs are cellular networks that provide wireless connectivity over large geographical areas, covering regions, countries, or even continents. They use mobile network infrastructure and technologies, such as 4G LTE and 5G, to enable mobile communication and internet access for users on the move.

Components of Wireless Networks

Wireless networks consist of various components that work together to facilitate wireless communication and data transmission. Some of the key components of wireless networks include:

- **Wireless Access Points (APs)**: APs are devices that serve as the central hub for wireless communication within a WLAN. They transmit and receive wireless signals, allowing devices to connect to the network and access network resources.
- **Wireless Network Interface Cards (NICs)**: NICs are hardware components installed in computers, laptops, and mobile devices to enable wireless connectivity. They communicate with APs and other wireless devices using radio waves, facilitating data transmission and reception over the wireless network.
- **Wireless Routers**: Wireless routers combine the functionality of a router, switch, and AP into a single device, providing wired and wireless connectivity to devices within a network. They manage network traffic, assign IP addresses, and provide firewall protection to secure the network.
- **Wireless Security Protocols**: Wireless networks employ various security protocols, such as WPA3, WPA2, and WEP, to encrypt wireless communications and protect sensitive data from unauthorized access and interception. These protocols ensure the confidentiality, integrity, and authenticity of wireless transmissions, safeguarding network resources and user privacy.

Key Concepts in Wireless Networks

Understanding key concepts in wireless networks is essential for grasping their operation principles and functionalities. Some of the fundamental concepts include:

- **SSID (Service Set Identifier)**: SSID is a unique identifier assigned to a wireless network to distinguish it from other networks in the vicinity. It serves as the network name that users select when connecting to a WLAN.

- **Frequency Bands**: Wireless networks operate on various frequency bands, such as 2.4 GHz and 5 GHz, to transmit data between devices. Different frequency bands offer distinct advantages in terms of coverage, speed, and interference mitigation.
- **Channel**: A channel is a specific frequency range within a frequency band used by wireless networks to transmit data. By selecting the optimal channel, network administrators can minimize interference and optimize network performance.
- **Authentication and Encryption**: Wireless networks use authentication mechanisms and encryption algorithms to verify the identity of users and secure data transmissions. Strong authentication and encryption protocols are essential for protecting against unauthorized access and data breaches.

Understanding the basics of wireless networks is fundamental for grasping their functionality, components, and operation principles, which are crucial for effective wireless network security management. By gaining insights into the types, components, and key concepts of wireless networks, individuals and organizations can develop a solid foundation for implementing and maintaining secure and resilient wireless environments.

As we continue to explore the fascinating world of wireless network security in the following sections, we will delve deeper into the intricacies of wireless technologies, vulnerabilities, threats, and best practices for securing wireless networks effectively.

5.2 Wireless Security Protocols

Wireless security protocols play a pivotal role in safeguarding wireless networks from various threats and vulnerabilities that can compromise the confidentiality, integrity, and availability of sensitive information and network resources. As wireless networks continue to proliferate across homes, businesses, and public spaces, implementing robust security protocols becomes imperative to ensure secure and reliable connectivity. In this section, we'll explore the most commonly used wireless security protocols, discussing their features, strengths, and vulnerabilities to help you make informed decisions for securing your wireless networks.

WEP (Wired Equivalent Privacy)

WEP (Wired Equivalent Privacy) was one of the first wireless security protocols introduced to encrypt wireless communications and protect sensitive data from unauthorized access. However, WEP has several significant vulnerabilities that make it susceptible to exploitation, including weak encryption algorithms and static encryption keys. Despite its obsolescence and lack of robust security features, some legacy devices and networks may still use WEP due to compatibility issues with older hardware.

WPA (Wi-Fi Protected Access)

WPA (Wi-Fi Protected Access) was introduced as a successor to WEP to address its security shortcomings and enhance wireless network security.

WPA employs stronger encryption algorithms, such as TKIP (Temporal Key Integrity Protocol) and AES (Advanced Encryption Standard), to encrypt wireless communications and protect data integrity. WPA also introduced dynamic encryption keys and improved authentication mechanisms, making it more resilient against various wireless attacks compared to WEP.

WPA2 (Wi-Fi Protected Access 2)

WPA2 (Wi-Fi Protected Access 2) is the current industry standard for wireless security protocols, offering enhanced security features and robust protection against modern wireless threats. WPA2 utilizes the AES encryption algorithm and introduces advanced security mechanisms, such as CCMP (Counter Mode with Cipher Block Chaining Message Authentication Code Protocol), to secure wireless communications effectively. WPA2 also supports enterprise-grade authentication methods, including 802.1X and RADIUS, for stronger user authentication and access control.

WPA3 (Wi-Fi Protected Access 3)

WPA3 (Wi-Fi Protected Access 3) is the latest iteration of the WPA security protocol, designed to address emerging security challenges and further enhance wireless network security. WPA3 introduces several new features and improvements, including:

- **Enhanced Encryption**: WPA3 introduces the Simultaneous Authentication of Equals (SAE) protocol, also known as

Dragonfly, to replace the pre-shared key (PSK) authentication method used in WPA2. SAE offers stronger protection against brute-force attacks and dictionary attacks, enhancing the security of wireless communications.

- **Forward Secrecy**: WPA3 incorporates forward secrecy by generating unique session keys for each connection, ensuring that compromising one session key does not compromise past or future sessions.
- **Protected Management Frames (PMF)**: WPA3 mandates the use of PMF to protect management frames from tampering and forgery, further securing the wireless network against various attacks, such as de-authentication attacks and frame injection attacks.

Choosing the Right Wireless Security Protocol

Selecting the right wireless security protocol depends on various factors, including the network environment, device compatibility, and security requirements. Here are some considerations to help you choose the appropriate wireless security protocol for your wireless network:

- **Upgrade to WPA3**: If your devices and network infrastructure support WPA3, consider upgrading to WPA3 to leverage its enhanced security features and protections against modern wireless threats.
- **Use WPA2 as a Minimum**: If WPA3 is not an option due to hardware limitations, use WPA2 as a minimum security standard and disable outdated and insecure protocols like WEP to mitigate known vulnerabilities and enhance wireless network security.

- **Implement Strong Authentication and Encryption**: Regardless of the security protocol used, ensure to implementation of strong authentication methods, such as complex passwords and multifactor authentication (MFA), and enable robust encryption algorithms like AES to protect wireless communications effectively.

Wireless security protocols are essential components of wireless network security, providing the necessary safeguards to protect against various threats and vulnerabilities. By understanding the features, strengths, and vulnerabilities of different wireless security protocols, individuals and organizations can make informed decisions for implementing and maintaining secure and resilient wireless environments.

As we continue to explore the fascinating world of wireless network security in the following sections, we will delve deeper into advanced techniques, best practices, and emerging trends in wireless security to help you master the art of securing wireless networks effectively and mitigating the risks associated with wireless technology.

5.3 Wireless Attacks and Countermeasures

Wireless networks, despite their convenience and ubiquity, are susceptible to a variety of attacks that can compromise their security and expose sensitive information to unauthorized access. Understanding these wireless attacks and implementing effective countermeasures is crucial for maintaining the integrity, confidentiality, and availability of wireless networks. In this section, we'll explore common wireless attacks and discuss proactive countermeasures to help you bolster the security of your wireless networks effectively.

Common Wireless Attacks

1. Eavesdropping (Sniffing)

Eavesdropping involves the unauthorized interception of wireless communications to capture sensitive information, such as passwords, credit card numbers, and personal data. Attackers use wireless sniffing tools to capture and analyze wireless traffic, exploiting weak security protocols and unencrypted connections to extract valuable information.

2. Man-in-the-Middle (MitM) Attacks

Man-in-the-middle (MitM) Attacks occur when attackers intercept and potentially alter communication between two parties without their knowledge. In wireless networks, MitM attacks can compromise the confidentiality and integrity of data transmissions by impersonating legitimate devices or intercepting data in transit.

3. Denial of Service (DoS) and Distributed Denial of Service (DDoS) Attacks

Denial of Service (DoS) and Distributed Denial of Service (DDoS) Attacks target wireless networks by flooding them with excessive traffic or malicious requests, causing network congestion, service disruption, and performance degradation. These attacks can render wireless networks inaccessible, disrupting critical operations and services.

4. Rogue Access Points and Evil Twins

Rogue Access Points and Evil Twins are unauthorized wireless access points deployed by attackers to lure unsuspecting users and capture sensitive information. These deceptive networks mimic legitimate SSIDs to deceive users into connecting, enabling attackers to intercept communications and launch further attacks on connected devices.

5. Brute-Force and Dictionary Attacks

Brute-force and Dictionary Attacks target wireless networks by attempting to guess or crack passwords and encryption keys through systematic trial-and-error methods. Attackers use specialized tools to automate password guessing and exploit weak authentication mechanisms to gain unauthorized access to network resources.

Proactive Countermeasures and Best Practices

1. Enable Strong Encryption and Authentication

Implement WPA3: Upgrade to WPA3 to leverage its advanced encryption and authentication features, such as the Simultaneous Authentication of Equals (SAE) protocol and forward secrecy, to protect against brute-force attacks, eavesdropping, and MitM attacks.

2. Secure Network Configuration and Management

- **Change Default Settings**: Modify default SSIDs, passwords, and administrative credentials to prevent unauthorized access and reduce the risk of exploitation.
- **Disable SSID Broadcasting**: Disable SSID broadcasting to make the wireless network less visible to potential attackers and reduce the risk of unauthorized connections.

3. Implement Network Segmentation and Isolation

- **Use VLANs**: Implement Virtual Local Area Networks (VLANs) to segregate wireless traffic from critical network resources, limiting the impact of potential compromises and containing security incidents.
- **Enable Client Isolation**: Enable client isolation features on wireless access points to prevent connected devices from communicating with each other, reducing the risk of lateral movement and unauthorized access.

4. Monitor and Detect Anomalies

- **Deploy IDS/IPS Solutions**: Deploy Intrusion Detection Systems (IDS) and Intrusion Prevention Systems (IPS) to monitor wireless traffic, detect suspicious activities, and mitigate potential security threats in real-time.
- **Enable Logging and Auditing**: Enable logging and auditing capabilities on wireless devices and network infrastructure to

maintain visibility into network activities, facilitate incident response, and support forensic investigations.

5. Educate and Train Users

Security Awareness Training: Educate users on wireless security best practices, such as avoiding public Wi-Fi networks, using strong passwords, and enabling multi-factor authentication (MFA), to mitigate the risks associated with wireless technology and promote a security-conscious culture.

Wireless networks are susceptible to a variety of attacks that can compromise their security and expose sensitive information to unauthorized access. By understanding common wireless attacks, implementing proactive countermeasures, and adopting security best practices, individuals and organizations can bolster the security of their wireless networks effectively and mitigate the risks associated with wireless technology.

As we continue to explore the fascinating world of wireless network security in the following sections, we will delve deeper into advanced techniques, tools, and strategies for securing wireless networks and defending against evolving wireless threats.

Chapter 6: Web Application Security

Web applications have become integral to our digital lives, providing us with convenient access to a multitude of services, from online banking and shopping to social networking and entertainment. However, the ubiquity and complexity of web applications make them prime targets for cybercriminals seeking to exploit vulnerabilities and compromise sensitive data. Ensuring the security of web applications is paramount to safeguarding user information, preserving trust, and maintaining the integrity of online services. In this chapter, we'll delve into the intricacies of web application security, exploring the challenges, vulnerabilities, and best practices to help you build and maintain secure web applications effectively.

1. Understanding Web Applications

Web applications are software programs that run on web servers and interact with users through web browsers over the internet. Unlike traditional desktop applications, web applications are accessible from any device with an internet connection, making them highly versatile and convenient. However, this accessibility also introduces unique security challenges due to the complex interplay of technologies involved, including web servers, databases, programming languages, and client-side scripts.

2. Common Web Application Vulnerabilities

Web applications are susceptible to a variety of vulnerabilities that can be exploited to compromise their security and expose sensitive data to unauthorized access. Understanding these vulnerabilities is crucial for identifying potential risks and implementing effective countermeasures. Some of the most common web application vulnerabilities include:

- **SQL Injection (SQLi)**: SQL injection attacks exploit inadequate input validation and improper handling of user-supplied input to execute malicious SQL queries against the underlying database, enabling attackers to retrieve, modify, or delete sensitive data.
- **Cross-Site Scripting (XSS)**: Cross-site scripting attacks involve injecting malicious scripts into web pages viewed by users, bypassing access controls, and exploiting vulnerabilities in web applications to steal session cookies, redirect users to malicious websites, or perform unauthorized actions on behalf of the user.
- **Cross-Site Request Forgery (CSRF)**: Cross-site request forgery attacks trick authenticated users into executing unintended actions on web applications by exploiting their inherent trust and leveraging their active sessions to perform unauthorized transactions or modify account settings.
- **Insecure Direct Object References (IDOR)**: Insecure direct object references occur when web applications expose internal implementation details, such as database keys or file paths, allowing attackers to manipulate parameters and access unauthorized resources or sensitive data.
- **Sensitive Data Exposure**: Sensitive data exposure vulnerabilities arise when web applications fail to adequately protect sensitive

information, such as passwords, credit card numbers, and personal data, through encryption, hashing, and secure storage practices.

3. Best Practices for Web Application Security

Implementing robust security measures and adhering to best practices are essential for mitigating web application vulnerabilities and ensuring the integrity, confidentiality, and availability of web applications. Here are some best practices to help you enhance web application security effectively:

- **Input Validation and Sanitization**: Implement rigorous input validation and sanitization routines to filter and sanitize user-supplied input, preventing SQL injection, XSS, and other injection attacks.
- **Parameterized Queries**: Use parameterized queries and prepared statements to interact with databases securely, reducing the risk of SQL injection attacks by separating SQL code from user input.
- **Content Security Policy (CSP)**: Implement a Content Security Policy (CSP) to mitigate XSS attacks by defining and enforcing a whitelist of trusted sources for loading resources, scripts, and stylesheets on web pages.
- **Session Management and Authentication**: Implement strong session management and authentication mechanisms, including secure session cookies, strong password policies, multi-factor authentication (MFA), and account lockout policies, to protect against unauthorized access and session hijacking.
- **Secure Communication**: Use secure communication protocols, such as HTTPS, to encrypt data in transit between clients and

servers, ensuring the confidentiality and integrity of sensitive information transmitted over the Internet.

- **Regular Security Audits and Penetration Testing**: Conduct regular security audits, vulnerability assessments, and penetration testing to identify and remediate security vulnerabilities, validate security controls, and ensure compliance with industry standards and regulations.

Web application security is a complex and multifaceted discipline that requires a proactive approach to identify, assess, and mitigate potential risks and vulnerabilities effectively. By understanding the nature of web applications, recognizing common vulnerabilities, and implementing robust security measures and best practices, individuals and organizations can build and maintain secure web applications that protect user information, preserve trust, and uphold the integrity of online services.

As we continue to explore the dynamic and challenging landscape of web application security in the following sections, we will delve deeper into advanced techniques, tools, and strategies for securing web applications and defending against evolving web-based threats and attacks.

6.1 Understanding Web Applications

Web applications have revolutionized the way we interact with the internet, offering dynamic and interactive experiences that range from simple blogs and e-commerce sites to complex enterprise systems and social media platforms. Understanding the fundamentals of web applications is crucial for grasping their architecture, functionalities, and potential security vulnerabilities. In this section, we'll delve into the intricacies of web applications, exploring their components, architecture, and the technologies that power them.

What is a Web Application?

A web application is a software program that resides on a web server and delivers interactive content to users via web browsers over the internet. Unlike static websites, which display fixed content stored in HTML files, web applications generate dynamic content in real time by processing user input, interacting with databases, and executing server-side scripts. This dynamic nature enables web applications to provide personalized and interactive experiences tailored to individual user preferences and actions.

Components of Web Applications

Web applications are composed of multiple components that work together to deliver seamless and engaging user experiences. Some of the key components of web applications include:

- **Client-Side Technologies**: Client-side technologies, such as HTML, CSS, and JavaScript, are responsible for rendering web pages in users' browsers and enabling interactive user interfaces. These technologies execute on the client's device, allowing web applications to respond to user input and deliver dynamic content without requiring server interactions for every action.
- **Server-Side Technologies**: Server-side technologies, such as PHP, Python, Ruby, Java, and .NET, handle the processing of user

requests, interact with databases, and generate dynamic content in response to client requests. These technologies execute on the web server, enabling web applications to perform complex computations, execute business logic, and interact with external services and resources.

- **Databases**: Databases store and manage the structured data used by web applications to maintain user profiles, store product information, manage inventory, and facilitate data-driven interactions. Common database systems used in web applications include MySQL, PostgreSQL, MongoDB, and Microsoft SQL Server.

- **Web Servers**: Web servers, such as Apache HTTP Server, Nginx, and Microsoft IIS, host and serve web applications to clients over the internet. They handle incoming HTTP requests, route requests to the appropriate application components, and deliver responses back to clients, ensuring smooth and reliable communication between users and web applications.

Web Application Architecture

Web applications typically follow a multi-tier architecture, often referred to as the three-tier architecture, which separates the application into three interconnected layers: the presentation layer, the business logic layer, and the data layer.

- **Presentation Layer**: The presentation layer, also known as the front end, is responsible for rendering the user interface and handling user interactions. It consists of client-side technologies, such as HTML, CSS, and JavaScript, which run in the user's browser and communicate with the server to request and display dynamic content.

- **Business Logic Layer**: The business logic layer, also known as the back-end, is responsible for processing user requests, executing application logic, and interacting with databases and external services. It consists of server-side technologies, such as PHP, Python, and Java, which run on the web server and handle the core functionality of the web application.

- **Data Layer**: The data layer is responsible for storing and managing the data used by the web application. It consists of databases, such as MySQL and MongoDB, which store structured data, facilitate data retrieval and manipulation, and ensure data integrity and consistency across the application.

Understanding web applications is essential for grasping their architecture, functionalities, and potential security vulnerabilities. By recognizing the components, technologies, and architecture that power web applications, individuals and organizations can develop a deeper understanding of how web applications work and how they can be secured effectively against various threats and vulnerabilities.

As we continue to explore the fascinating world of web application security in the following sections, we will delve deeper into the intricacies of web application development, vulnerabilities, best practices, and security measures to help you build, maintain, and secure web applications effectively.

6.2 Common Web Application Vulnerabilities

Web applications, due to their dynamic and interactive nature, are susceptible to a wide range of vulnerabilities that can be exploited by malicious actors to compromise their security, steal sensitive data, and disrupt services. Understanding these common web application vulnerabilities is essential for identifying potential risks and implementing effective security measures to safeguard web applications from exploitation. In this section, we'll explore some of the most prevalent web application vulnerabilities, their underlying causes, and the potential impact they can have on web application security.

1. SQL Injection (SQLi)

SQL Injection (SQLi) is a type of attack that exploits inadequate input validation and improper handling of user-supplied input in web applications to execute malicious SQL queries against the underlying database. Attackers can manipulate input fields, such as login forms or search queries, to inject malicious SQL code, enabling them to retrieve, modify, or delete sensitive data stored in the database.

Impact: SQL injection attacks can lead to unauthorized access to sensitive information, data leakage, data corruption, and potential loss of user trust and reputation damage.

2. Cross-Site Scripting (XSS)

Cross-site scripting (XSS) is a type of attack that involves injecting malicious scripts into web pages viewed by users, bypassing access controls and exploiting vulnerabilities in web applications to steal session cookies, redirect users to malicious websites, or perform unauthorized actions on behalf of the user. XSS attacks can be categorized into three types: Stored XSS, Reflected XSS, and DOM-based XSS, depending on how the malicious script is delivered and executed.

Impact: XSS attacks can compromise user accounts, steal sensitive information, facilitate session hijacking, and enable further exploitation of web application vulnerabilities.

3. Cross-Site Request Forgery (CSRF)

Cross-Site Request Forgery (CSRF) is a type of attack that tricks authenticated users into executing unintended actions on web applications by exploiting their inherent trust and leveraging their active sessions to perform unauthorized transactions or modify account settings. Attackers can craft malicious requests, such as form submissions or URL parameters, to exploit CSRF vulnerabilities and manipulate user actions without their knowledge.

Impact: CSRF attacks can lead to unauthorized transactions, account takeover, data manipulation, and potential financial losses for users and organizations.

4. Insecure Direct Object References (IDOR)

Insecure Direct Object References (IDOR) occur when web applications expose internal implementation details, such as database keys or file paths, allowing attackers to manipulate parameters and access unauthorized resources or sensitive data. Attackers can modify parameters in URLs, forms, or API requests to bypass access controls and gain unauthorized access to restricted resources.

Impact: IDOR vulnerabilities can lead to unauthorized data access, information disclosure, privilege escalation, and potential compromise of sensitive information.

5. Security Misconfigurations

Security Misconfigurations refer to insecure configurations and settings in web applications, web servers, databases, and other components that expose vulnerabilities and weaken overall security posture. Common examples include default credentials, open ports, directory listings, and unnecessary services that can be exploited by attackers to gain unauthorized access and compromise web application security.

Impact: Security misconfigurations can lead to unauthorized access, data exposure, service disruptions, and potential exploitation of vulnerabilities to compromise web applications and underlying infrastructure.

Web application vulnerabilities pose significant risks to the security and integrity of web applications, potentially exposing sensitive information, compromising user accounts, and facilitating unauthorized access and data manipulation. By understanding the nature of common web application vulnerabilities, their underlying causes, and the potential impact they can have on web application security, individuals and organizations can take proactive measures to identify, assess, and mitigate these vulnerabilities effectively.

In the following sections, we will delve deeper into best practices, security measures, and mitigation strategies to help you build, maintain, and secure web applications against these common vulnerabilities and emerging threats.

6.3 Tools for Web Application Penetration Testing

Web application penetration testing, commonly referred to as web app pen testing, is a crucial process for identifying and assessing vulnerabilities in web applications to ensure their security and resilience against potential cyber threats. Leveraging specialized tools designed for web app pen testing can streamline the testing process, automate vulnerability discovery, and facilitate effective remediation efforts. In this section, we'll explore some of the most popular and widely used tools for web application penetration testing, highlighting their features, capabilities, and how they can be utilized to enhance web application security.

1. Burp Suite

Burp Suite is a leading web application testing toolkit widely used by security professionals and penetration testers to identify and exploit vulnerabilities in web applications. It offers a comprehensive set of tools, including an intercepting proxy, web vulnerability scanner, intruder, repeater, and sequencer, to facilitate manual and automated testing of web applications. Burp Suite enables users to intercept, modify, and analyze HTTP requests and responses, identify security flaws, and validate the effectiveness of security controls.

Features:

- Intercepting Proxy
- Web Vulnerability Scanner
- Intruder
- Repeater
- Sequencer
- Extensibility with custom plugins

2. OWASP ZAP (Zed Attack Proxy)

OWASP ZAP (Zed Attack Proxy) is an open-source web application security testing tool designed to identify security vulnerabilities in web applications and APIs. It offers a user-friendly interface and a range of automated scanners and tools to help users identify common web application vulnerabilities, such as SQL injection, XSS, CSRF, and insecure configurations. OWASP ZAP also provides advanced features, including active and passive scanning modes, fuzzing, and automated vulnerability detection and reporting.

Features:

- Automated Scanning
- Active and Passive Scanning Modes
- Fuzzing
- AJAX Spider
- API Testing

- Reporting and Alerting

3. Nikto

Nikto is an open-source web server scanner that performs comprehensive vulnerability assessments and identifies potential security issues in web servers and web applications. It scans web servers for misconfigurations, outdated software, known vulnerabilities, and common security weaknesses that can be exploited by attackers. Nikto supports a wide range of web server platforms and technologies, making it a versatile tool for conducting initial reconnaissance and identifying potential attack vectors.

Features:

- Comprehensive Web Server Scanning
- Outdated Software Detection
- Known Vulnerability Identification
- SSL/TLS Security Checks
- Reporting and Logging

4. SQLMap

SQLMap is a powerful open-source penetration testing tool that automates the process of detecting and exploiting SQL injection vulnerabilities in web applications and databases. It supports various database systems, including MySQL, PostgreSQL, Oracle, and

Microsoft SQL Server, and offers a range of advanced features to facilitate SQL injection detection, exploitation, and post-exploitation activities. SQLMap enables users to perform database fingerprinting, data retrieval, privilege escalation, and execute arbitrary SQL queries through a user-friendly command-line interface.

Features:

- Automated SQL Injection Detection
- Database Fingerprinting
- Data Retrieval and Dumping
- Privilege Escalation
- Post-Exploitation Activities

Web application penetration testing is a critical component of an effective web application security strategy, enabling organizations to identify, assess, and remediate vulnerabilities before they can be exploited by malicious actors. Leveraging specialized tools for web application penetration testing can enhance the efficiency, accuracy, and comprehensiveness of security assessments, empowering organizations to build and maintain secure web applications that protect sensitive data, preserve user trust, and comply with regulatory requirements.

As we continue to explore the dynamic and challenging realm of web application security in the following sections, we will delve deeper into advanced techniques, best practices, and strategies for securing web applications and defending against evolving web-based threats and attacks.

Chapter 7: System Hacking

System hacking is a term that encompasses a broad range of activities aimed at exploiting vulnerabilities in computer systems, networks, and software applications to gain unauthorized access, escalate privileges, and compromise the integrity, confidentiality, and availability of data and resources. Understanding the techniques, tools, and strategies employed by hackers to compromise systems is essential for implementing robust security measures and safeguarding against potential cyber threats. In this chapter, we'll delve into the fascinating world of system hacking, exploring the methodologies, vulnerabilities, and countermeasures to help you fortify your systems against malicious attacks effectively.

1. Understanding System Hacking

System hacking involves exploiting weaknesses in computer systems, networks, and software applications through various techniques, such as exploiting software vulnerabilities, brute-force attacks, password cracking, and social engineering, to gain unauthorized access and control over targeted systems. Hackers employ a combination of technical skills, knowledge of system architectures, and sophisticated tools to identify, exploit, and manipulate security flaws and weaknesses in systems to achieve their objectives.

2. Common System Hacking Techniques

- **Password Cracking**

Password cracking is a technique used by hackers to decipher passwords through various methods, such as brute-force attacks, dictionary attacks, and rainbow table attacks. Hackers utilize specialized tools and algorithms to automate password guessing and cracking processes, exploiting weak passwords and inadequate password policies to gain unauthorized access to user accounts and systems.

- **Malware and Exploits**

Malware and exploits are malicious software programs and code snippets designed to exploit vulnerabilities in systems and applications to compromise their security and facilitate unauthorized access and control. Hackers distribute malware through phishing emails, malicious websites, and compromised networks to infect systems, steal sensitive information, and create backdoors for remote access and control.

- **Social Engineering**

Social engineering involves manipulating individuals through psychological manipulation and deception techniques to trick them into revealing sensitive information, such as passwords, access credentials, and confidential data. Hackers exploit human vulnerabilities and trust to bypass security controls, gain unauthorized access to systems, and facilitate targeted attacks and data breaches.

3. Man-in-the-Middle (MitM) Attacks

Man-in-the-middle (MitM) attacks occur when attackers intercept and potentially alter communication between two parties without their knowledge. Hackers exploit insecure communication channels and protocols to eavesdrop on sensitive information, capture session cookies, and redirect traffic to malicious websites, compromising the confidentiality and integrity of data transmissions.

Countermeasures and Best Practices

Implementing robust security measures and best practices is essential for mitigating system hacking risks and safeguarding systems against potential cyber threats. Here are some countermeasures and best practices to help you fortify your systems effectively:

1. Strong Authentication and Access Control

- **Implement Strong Password Policies**: Enforce complex password requirements, multi-factor authentication (MFA), and regular password updates to enhance user account security and mitigate password cracking risks.
- **Role-Based Access Control (RBAC)**: Implement RBAC to enforce least privilege access and restrict user permissions based

on roles and responsibilities, limiting the impact of potential compromises and unauthorized access.

2. Regular Software Updates and Patch Management

- **Apply Security Patches**: Regularly update and patch operating systems, software applications, and firmware to address known vulnerabilities and protect systems against malware, exploits, and zero-day attacks.
- **Vulnerability Management**: Conduct regular vulnerability assessments and penetration testing to identify and remediate security vulnerabilities proactively, ensuring the integrity and security of systems and applications.

3. Security Awareness and Training

- **Employee Training**: Educate employees on system hacking risks, social engineering tactics, and cybersecurity best practices to foster a security-conscious culture, enhance awareness, and reduce the likelihood of human errors and mistakes.
- **Phishing Simulations**: Conduct phishing simulations and awareness campaigns to simulate real-world attack scenarios, assess employee readiness, and reinforce cybersecurity awareness and vigilance.

4. Network Security and Monitoring

- **Network Segmentation**: Implement network segmentation and isolation to separate critical assets and resources, limit lateral movement, and contain potential compromises to specific network segments.
- **Network Monitoring and Intrusion Detection**: Deploy network monitoring tools, intrusion detection systems (IDS), and intrusion prevention systems (IPS) to monitor network traffic, detect suspicious activities, and respond to security incidents in real time.

System hacking poses significant risks to the security and integrity of computer systems, networks, and data, potentially leading to unauthorized access, data breaches, financial losses, and reputational damage. By understanding the methodologies, vulnerabilities, and techniques employed by hackers to compromise systems, and implementing robust security measures, best practices, and countermeasures, individuals and organizations can fortify their systems effectively and safeguard against potential cyber threats and attacks.

As we continue to explore the dynamic and challenging landscape of cybersecurity in the following chapters, we will delve deeper into advanced techniques, tools, and strategies for securing systems, networks, and applications and defending against evolving cyber threats and attack vectors.

7.1 Windows and Linux Security

Windows and Linux are two of the most widely used operating systems (OS) in the world, each with its unique architecture, features, and security considerations. Ensuring the security of Windows and Linux systems is essential for protecting data, applications, and resources from unauthorized access, malware infections, and other cyber threats. In this section, we'll explore the security features, vulnerabilities, and best practices for securing Windows and Linux systems effectively.

Windows Security

Windows is a popular operating system developed by Microsoft, commonly used in desktops, laptops, and servers. Microsoft has incorporated various security features and enhancements over the years to improve the overall security posture of Windows systems. Here are some key security features and best practices for securing Windows systems:

Security Features:

- **User Account Control (UAC)**: UAC prompts users for permission or an administrator password before allowing applications to make changes that could potentially impact system settings or install malware, providing an additional layer of security against unauthorized changes and malware infections.
- **Windows Defender Antivirus**: Windows Defender is a built-in antivirus and antimalware solution that provides real-time

protection against viruses, malware, and other malicious threats, helping to safeguard Windows systems from common cyber threats.

- **BitLocker Drive Encryption**: BitLocker is a full-disk encryption feature that encrypts the entire hard drive to protect data from unauthorized access, theft, and exposure in case of loss or theft of the device.

Best Practices:

- **Regular Updates and Patch Management**: Enable automatic updates and regularly install security patches, updates, and hotfixes provided by Microsoft to address known vulnerabilities and protect Windows systems against malware, exploits, and security weaknesses.
- **Strong Password Policies and Authentication**: Implement strong password policies, multi-factor authentication (MFA), and account lockout policies to enhance user account security, mitigate password cracking risks, and prevent unauthorized access to Windows systems.
- **Firewall and Network Security**: Enable Windows Firewall and configure advanced security settings to monitor and control incoming and outgoing network traffic, restrict unauthorized access to services and applications, and protect Windows systems from network-based attacks and threats.

Linux Security

Linux is an open-source operating system based on the Unix-like kernel, widely used in servers, embedded systems, and various computing devices. Linux offers robust security features and flexibility, allowing users to customize and optimize security configurations based on specific requirements and use cases. Here are some key security features and best practices for securing Linux systems:

Security Features:

- **User and Group Management**: Linux utilizes a robust user and group management system to control access permissions, privileges, and resource allocation, enabling administrators to enforce least privilege access and enhance system security.
- **SELinux and AppArmor**: Security-Enhanced Linux (SELinux) and AppArmor are mandatory access control (MAC) security mechanisms that enforce strict policies and restrictions on system resources, applications, and services to prevent unauthorized access, privilege escalation, and malicious activities.
- **Firewall and IPTables**: Linux provides built-in firewall solutions, such as IPTables and firewalld, to filter and control network traffic, manage incoming and outgoing connections, and protect Linux systems from network-based attacks, unauthorized access, and malicious activities.

Best Practices:

- **Regular Updates and Patch Management**: Keep Linux systems up-to-date with the latest security patches, updates, and fixes provided by Linux distributions and package managers to address known vulnerabilities, and security weaknesses, and protect against emerging threats and exploits.
- **Secure Configuration and Hardening**: Implement secure configurations and hardening measures, such as disabling unnecessary services, restricting root access, enabling secure boot, and configuring file and directory permissions, to reduce the attack surface, minimize security risks, and enhance the overall security posture of Linux systems.
- **Monitoring and Logging**: Enable and configure system logging, auditing, and monitoring tools, such as syslog, auditd, and monitoring solutions, to track and analyze system activities, detect suspicious behaviors, and respond to security incidents and anomalies in real time.

Securing Windows and Linux systems is crucial for protecting data, applications, and resources from cyber threats, unauthorized access, and malicious activities. By understanding the security features, vulnerabilities, and best practices for Windows and Linux systems, administrators and users can implement robust security measures, configurations, and controls to mitigate risks, enhance system security, and maintain the integrity, confidentiality, and availability of systems and data.

As we continue to explore the dynamic and challenging landscape of cybersecurity in the following chapters, we will delve deeper into advanced techniques, tools, and strategies for securing systems, networks, and applications and defending against evolving cyber threats and attack vectors.

7.2 System Hardening Techniques

System hardening is the process of enhancing the security of a computer system by reducing its attack surface, eliminating unnecessary services and functionalities, and implementing robust security configurations and controls to mitigate risks and vulnerabilities. Hardening a system involves a series of steps and best practices aimed at strengthening the overall security posture of the system against potential cyber threats and attacks. In this section, we'll explore various system hardening techniques and best practices that can be applied to both Windows and Linux systems to enhance their security effectively.

General System Hardening Techniques

1. **Disable Unnecessary Services and Protocols**

- **Identify and Disable Unnecessary Services**: Review and identify unnecessary services, protocols, and applications running on the system and disable or remove them to reduce the attack surface and potential vulnerabilities.
- **Configure Firewall Rules**: Implement firewall rules to block incoming and outgoing traffic for unnecessary services and protocols, restricting access and minimizing exposure to potential threats and attacks.

2. Update and Patch Management

- **Enable Automatic Updates**: Enable automatic updates and regularly install security patches, updates, and hotfixes provided by the OS vendor and software developers to address known vulnerabilities and protect the system against exploits and malware infections.
- **Regular System Scans**: Conduct regular vulnerability scans and assessments using security tools and solutions to identify and remediate security weaknesses, misconfigurations, and potential risks proactively.

3. User Account Management and Privilege Control

- **Implement the Least Privilege Principle**: Enforce least privilege access and restrict user permissions, privileges, and capabilities based on roles and responsibilities to limit the impact of potential compromises and unauthorized access.
- **Enable Multi-factor Authentication (MFA)**: Implement MFA for user accounts, administrative access, and critical system operations to enhance authentication security, mitigate password-related risks, and prevent unauthorized access and account compromise.

4. Secure Configurations and Hardening Measures

- **Secure Boot and BIOS/UEFI Settings**: Enable secure boot and configure BIOS/UEFI settings to prevent unauthorized modifications, tampering, and boot-level attacks, ensuring the integrity and security of the system startup process.

- **File and Directory Permissions**: Configure file and directory permissions, ownership, and access controls to restrict unauthorized access, prevent data leakage, and protect sensitive system files and directories from unauthorized modifications and tampering.

Windows System Hardening Techniques

1. **Windows Security Features and Policies**

- **Enable BitLocker Encryption**: Implement BitLocker drive encryption to protect sensitive data, files, and system partitions from unauthorized access, theft, and exposure in case of loss or theft of the device.
- **Configure Group Policy Settings**: Utilize Group Policy settings to enforce security policies, restrictions, and configurations across Windows systems, ensuring consistent security posture and compliance with organizational and regulatory requirements.

2. **Windows Defender and Security Tools**

- **Enable Windows Defender Antivirus**: Activate Windows Defender Antivirus to provide real-time protection against viruses, malware, and other malicious threats, safeguarding Windows systems from common cyber threats and infections.

- **Utilize Microsoft Baseline Security Analyzer (MBSA)**: Use MBSA to scan and assess the security state of Windows systems, identify missing security updates, patches, and misconfigurations, and remediate vulnerabilities to improve the overall security posture of Windows environments.

Linux System Hardening Techniques

1. SELinux and AppArmor Policies

- **Configure SELinux Policies**: Implement and configure SELinux policies to enforce strict access controls, restrictions, and permissions on system resources, applications, and services, preventing unauthorized access, privilege escalation, and malicious activities.
- **Utilize AppArmor Profiles**: Deploy and manage AppArmor profiles to confine applications, limit capabilities, and enforce security policies on specific applications and processes, reducing the attack surface and mitigating the impact of potential compromises and vulnerabilities.

2. Secure Network and Firewall Configuration

- **Implement IPTables Rules**: Configure IPTables rules and settings to filter and control network traffic, manage incoming and outgoing connections, and protect Linux systems from network-based attacks, unauthorized access, and malicious activities.

- **Secure SSH and Remote Access**: Harden SSH configurations, disable root login, implement key-based authentication, and restrict remote access to trusted IPs and networks to enhance the security of remote access and protect against brute-force attacks and unauthorized access attempts.

System hardening is a critical component of an effective cybersecurity strategy, enabling organizations and individuals to strengthen the security of their systems, protect sensitive data and resources, and defend against potential cyber threats and attacks. By implementing robust system hardening techniques, best practices, and security controls, administrators and users can mitigate risks, reduce vulnerabilities, and maintain the integrity, confidentiality, and availability of systems and data effectively.

As we continue to explore the dynamic and challenging landscape of cybersecurity in the following chapters, we will delve deeper into advanced techniques, tools, and strategies for securing systems, networks, and applications and defending against evolving cyber threats and attack vectors.

7.3 Malware and Rootkits

Malware and rootkits represent two significant categories of malicious software designed to compromise the security, integrity, and functionality of computer systems, networks, and data. Understanding the nature, characteristics, and behavior of malware and rootkits is crucial for implementing effective security measures, detection mechanisms, and mitigation strategies to safeguard systems against these sophisticated cyber threats. In this section, we'll explore the concepts of malware and rootkits, their types, characteristics, detection methods, and best practices for protection and prevention.

Malware: Types and Characteristics

Malware, short for "malicious software," is a broad category of malicious programs designed to infiltrate, damage, or gain unauthorized access to computer systems, networks, and data. Malware encompasses various types and forms, each with its unique characteristics, capabilities, and objectives. Here are some common types of malware:

1. Viruses

Characteristics: Viruses are malicious programs that infect and modify legitimate files, programs, and systems to replicate themselves and spread to other systems through infected files, email attachments, and removable media.

2. Worms

Characteristics: Worms are standalone malware programs that replicate and spread across networks and systems without user intervention, exploiting vulnerabilities and weaknesses to propagate and infect targeted systems.

3. Trojans

Characteristics: Trojans are deceptive malware programs disguised as legitimate software or applications to trick users into downloading and executing them, enabling attackers to gain unauthorized access, steal sensitive information, and perform malicious activities.

4. Ransomware

Characteristics: Ransomware is a type of malware that encrypts files and data on infected systems, rendering them inaccessible, and demands ransom payments from victims in exchange for decryption keys and data recovery.

5. Spyware and Adware

Characteristics: Spyware and adware are malicious programs designed to monitor user activities, gather sensitive information, display unwanted advertisements, and track user behavior for advertising and marketing purposes without consent.

Rootkits: Types and Characteristics

Rootkits are stealthy and sophisticated malicious software programs designed to conceal the presence and activities of malware, attackers, and unauthorized users on compromised systems. Rootkits operate at a low-level of the operating system, manipulating system calls, processes, and data structures to evade detection, maintain persistence, and grant privileged access to attackers. Here are some common types of rootkits:

1. Kernel Mode Rootkits

Characteristics: Kernel mode rootkits operate at the kernel level of the operating system, intercepting system calls, modifying system structures, and bypassing security mechanisms to gain privileged access, conceal malicious activities, and maintain persistence on compromised systems.

2. User Mode Rootkits

Characteristics: User mode rootkits operate at the user level of the operating system, manipulating system processes, files, and configurations to hide malicious programs, evade detection, and maintain unauthorized access and control over compromised systems.

3. Bootkits

Characteristics: Bootkits are specialized rootkits designed to infect and compromise the system boot process, boot loaders, and firmware to gain control during system startup, bypass security controls, and establish persistent and stealthy presence on infected systems.

Detection and Prevention

- ## Malware Detection

Antivirus and Antimalware Solutions: Deploy and maintain robust antivirus and antimalware solutions to scan, detect, and remove malicious programs, viruses, worms, trojans, ransomware, and other malware types from infected systems and networks.

Behavioral Analysis and Heuristic Scanning: Utilize behavioral analysis and heuristic scanning techniques to identify and block suspicious activities, anomalous behaviors, and previously unknown malware variants based on patterns, characteristics, and behaviors.

- ## Rootkit Detection

Rootkit Scanning and Removal Tools: Utilize specialized rootkit scanning and removal tools, such as GMER, Rootkit Revealer, and rkhunter, to detect, analyze, and remove rootkits from infected systems by scanning memory, files, and system configurations for malicious artifacts and indicators of compromise.

Secure Boot and System Integrity: Enable secure boot, BIOS/UEFI protections, and system integrity features to prevent rootkits from tampering with the boot process, firmware, and system configurations, ensuring the integrity and security of system startup and operations.

Malware and rootkits pose significant risks to the security, integrity, and functionality of computer systems, networks, and data, potentially leading to unauthorized access, data breaches, financial losses, and reputational damage. By understanding the characteristics, behaviors, and detection methods of malware and rootkits, and implementing robust security measures, best practices, and preventive controls, organizations and individuals can mitigate risks, protect sensitive information, and maintain the integrity, confidentiality, and availability of systems and data effectively.

As we continue to explore the dynamic and challenging landscape of cybersecurity in the following chapters, we will delve deeper into advanced techniques, tools, and strategies for securing systems, networks, and applications, and defending against evolving cyber threats and attack vectors.

Chapter 8: Network Security

Network security is a critical aspect of cybersecurity that focuses on safeguarding the integrity, confidentiality, and availability of data and resources within computer networks from unauthorized access, malicious attacks, and potential breaches. As networks continue to evolve and expand, the complexity and diversity of threats and vulnerabilities also increase, requiring comprehensive and adaptive security strategies, solutions, and practices to protect against a wide range of cyber threats and attacks. In this chapter, we'll delve into the fundamentals of network security, exploring key concepts, principles, technologies, and best practices to help you build and maintain secure and resilient networks effectively.

1. Fundamentals of Network Security

Network security encompasses a variety of technologies, processes, and practices designed to protect networked systems, devices, and data from unauthorized access, intrusions, and potential threats. Understanding the fundamentals of network security is essential for identifying risks, implementing appropriate security controls, and maintaining a secure and reliable network infrastructure. Here are some key concepts and principles of network security:

- **Confidentiality**

Definition: Confidentiality ensures that sensitive data, information, and communications are accessible and disclosed only to authorize users, preventing unauthorized access, eavesdropping, and data exposure.

- **Integrity**

Definition: Integrity ensures that data, information, and communications are accurate, complete, and unaltered during transmission and storage, safeguarding against unauthorized modifications, tampering, and data corruption.

- **Availability**

Definition: Availability ensures that network resources, services, and applications are accessible and operational when needed, minimizing downtime, disruptions, and service interruptions caused by cyber threats, attacks, and failures.

2. Common Network Security Threats

Understanding the types of threats and vulnerabilities targeting networks is crucial for identifying potential risks, assessing security postures, and implementing appropriate security measures and controls to mitigate and prevent attacks effectively. Here are some common network security threats:

Malware and Ransomware Attacks

- **Types**: Viruses, worms, trojans, ransomware

- **Impact**: Data breaches, data loss, financial losses, service disruptions

Phishing and Social Engineering Attacks

- **Types**: Phishing emails, spear phishing, whaling, pretexting
- **Impact**: Unauthorized access, account compromise, data theft, identity theft

Denial of Service (DoS) and Distributed Denial of Service (DDoS) Attacks

- **Types**: DoS attacks, DDoS attacks
- **Impact**: Service interruptions, network congestion, resource exhaustion

Man-in-the-Middle (MitM) Attacks

- **Types**: Session hijacking, SSL/TLS interception, DNS spoofing
- **Impact**: Data interception, eavesdropping, unauthorized access

3. Network Security Technologies and Solutions

Implementing robust network security technologies and solutions is essential for protecting networked systems, devices, and data from cyber threats, attacks, and potential breaches. Here are some essential network security technologies and solutions:

- **Firewalls**

Purpose: Control and monitor incoming and outgoing network traffic, filter traffic based on predefined rules and prevent unauthorized access to network resources and services.

- **Intrusion Detection and Prevention Systems (IDPS)**

Purpose: Monitor and analyze network traffic, detect suspicious activities and anomalies, and respond to potential threats and attacks in real time by blocking malicious traffic and alerts.

- **Virtual Private Networks (VPN)**

Purpose: Establish secure and encrypted connections over public networks, such as the Internet, to protect data transmission, communication, and remote access to network resources and services.

- **Secure Wi-Fi and Wireless Security Protocols**

Purpose: Secure wireless networks, implement authentication and encryption mechanisms, and protect against unauthorized access, eavesdropping, and network attacks targeting wireless communications and devices.

Best Practices for Network Security

Implementing best practices for network security is essential for maintaining a secure, resilient, and reliable network infrastructure that protects against a wide range of cyber threats and attacks. Here are some recommended best practices for network security:

- **Network Segmentation and Access Control**

Implement: Segregate network resources, devices, and services into separate network segments, enforce access controls, and restrict network traffic to authorized users and systems.

- **Regular Updates and Patch Management**

Implement: Keep network devices, systems, and software up-to-date with the latest security patches, updates, and fixes provided by vendors to address known vulnerabilities and protect against exploits and malware.

- **Strong Authentication and Password Policies**

Implement: Enforce strong authentication methods, multi-factor authentication (MFA), and complex password policies to enhance user account security, mitigate password-related risks, and prevent unauthorized access.

- **Network Monitoring, Logging, and Incident Response**

Implement: Deploy network monitoring tools, log management solutions, and incident response capabilities to monitor network activities, detect suspicious behaviors, and respond to security incidents and anomalies effectively.

Network security is a critical component of an effective cybersecurity strategy, encompassing a variety of technologies, practices, and measures designed to protect networked systems, devices, and data from unauthorized access, intrusions, and potential threats. By understanding the fundamentals of network security, identifying common threats, implementing robust security technologies and solutions, and adopting best practices, organizations and individuals can build and maintain secure, resilient, and reliable network infrastructures that safeguard against evolving cyber threats and attacks effectively.

As we continue to explore the dynamic and challenging landscape of cybersecurity in the following chapters, we will delve deeper into advanced techniques, tools, and strategies for securing systems, networks, and applications and defending against evolving cyber threats and attack vectors.

8.1 Firewalls and Intrusion Detection Systems

Firewalls and Intrusion Detection Systems (IDS) are fundamental components of network security infrastructure, playing pivotal roles in protecting networks from unauthorized access, malicious activities, and potential threats. Firewalls act as barriers between trusted internal networks and untrusted external networks, controlling and monitoring incoming and outgoing network traffic based on predefined security rules and policies. IDS, on the other hand, continuously monitors network activities, detects suspicious behaviors and anomalies, and alerts administrators to potential security incidents and breaches. In this section, we'll explore the concepts, functionalities, types, and best practices of firewalls and IDS to help you understand their significance and implementation in network security.

Firewalls: Concepts and Functionalities

A firewall is a network security device or software solution designed to monitor, filter, and control incoming and outgoing network traffic based on predetermined security rules, policies, and protocols. Firewalls create a barrier between trusted internal networks, such as private corporate networks, and untrusted external networks, such as the Internet, to protect network resources, services, and data from unauthorized access, intrusions, and potential threats. Here are the primary functionalities and capabilities of firewalls:

1. Packet Filtering

Function: Filter and inspect individual packets of data based on predefined rules, such as source and destination IP addresses, ports, and protocols, to allow or deny network traffic and protect against unauthorized access and malicious activities.

2. Stateful Inspection

Function: Track and analyze the state and context of network connections and sessions, including the source and destination addresses, ports, and protocols, to make informed decisions and enforce security policies based on the overall context and behavior of network traffic.

3. Application Layer Filtering

Function: Inspect and filter network traffic at the application layer, examining the content, structure, and behavior of application protocols and data to identify and block malicious activities, exploits, and attacks targeting specific applications and services.

Types of Firewalls

Firewalls can be classified into various types based on their deployment, functionalities, and architectural designs. Here are some common types of firewalls:

1. Network Firewalls

Type: Traditional hardware-based firewalls

Function: Protect network boundaries and segmentations, control and monitor network traffic between internal and external networks, and enforce security policies and access controls based on IP addresses, ports, and protocols.

2. Host-based Firewalls

Type: Software-based firewalls

Function: Protect individual devices, such as computers, servers, and mobile devices, control and filter incoming and outgoing traffic based on application-level rules, and provide an additional layer of defense against local threats and malware.

3. Next-Generation Firewalls (NGFW)

Type: Advanced hardware or software-based firewalls

Function: Combine traditional firewall functionalities with advanced capabilities, such as deep packet inspection (DPI), application awareness, and threat intelligence, to provide enhanced visibility, control, and protection against sophisticated cyber threats and attacks.

Intrusion Detection Systems (IDS): Concepts and Functionalities

An Intrusion Detection System (IDS) is a network security solution designed to monitor and analyze network activities, detect suspicious behaviors and anomalies, and alert administrators to potential security incidents and breaches in real-time. IDS operates by collecting and analyzing network traffic, logs, and events using predefined signatures, patterns, and algorithms to identify and respond to security threats and attacks effectively. Here are the primary functionalities and capabilities of IDS:

1. Signature-based Detection

Function: Compare network activities, events, and behaviors against known signatures, patterns, and indicators of known threats, attacks, and vulnerabilities to identify and alert on malicious activities and security incidents.

2. Anomaly-based Detection

Function: Establish baseline profiles and behavior patterns of normal network activities and behaviors, monitor and analyze deviations, anomalies, and irregularities in network traffic and events to detect and alert on suspicious activities and potential security breaches.

3. Real-time Monitoring and Alerts

Function: Continuously monitor, analyze, and correlate network traffic, events, and activities in real-time, generate alerts, notifications, and reports on detected security incidents, anomalies, and potential threats to facilitate timely response, investigation, and mitigation.

Firewalls and Intrusion Detection Systems (IDS) are essential components of network security infrastructure, providing critical capabilities and functionalities to protect networks from unauthorized access, malicious activities, and potential threats effectively. By understanding the concepts, functionalities, types, and best practices of firewalls and IDS, organizations and individuals can implement robust network security strategies, solutions, and controls to safeguard network resources, services, and data against evolving cyber threats and attack vectors.

As we continue to explore the dynamic and challenging landscape of cybersecurity in the following chapters, we will delve deeper into advanced techniques, tools, and strategies for securing systems, networks, and applications and defending against evolving cyber threats and attack vectors.

8.2 Virtual Private Networks (VPNs)

Virtual Private Networks (VPNs) have become an integral part of modern network security infrastructure, offering secure and encrypted connections over public networks, such as the Internet, to protect data transmission, communication, and remote access to network resources and services. VPNs enable organizations and individuals to establish private and secure connections across untrusted networks, ensuring confidentiality, integrity, and availability of data and communications. In this section, we'll delve into the concepts, functionalities, types, benefits, and best practices of VPNs to help you understand their significance and implementation in network security.

VPNs: Concepts and Functionalities

A Virtual Private Network (VPN) is a network technology that creates a secure and encrypted connection, often referred to as a tunnel, between a user's device and a remote network or server, allowing users to access network resources, services, and applications securely over the Internet. VPNs utilize various encryption protocols, authentication methods, and tunneling techniques to ensure the confidentiality, integrity, and authenticity of data and communications. Here are the primary functionalities and capabilities of VPNs:

1. Secure Data Transmission

Function: Encrypt data packets and communications between VPN clients and servers using strong encryption algorithms and protocols, such as SSL/TLS, IPSec, and OpenVPN, to protect against eavesdropping, data interception, and man-in-the-middle attacks.

2. Remote Access and Connectivity

Function: Enable remote users, employees, and partners to securely access and connect to internal networks, resources, and applications from remote locations, such as home offices, branch offices, and public Wi-Fi networks, without compromising security and privacy.

3. Anonymity and Privacy

Function: Mask and hide users' IP addresses, locations, and online activities by routing traffic through VPN servers and tunnels, providing anonymity, privacy, and protection against tracking, surveillance, and monitoring by ISPs, governments, and cybercriminals.

Types of VPNs

VPNs can be classified into various types based on their deployment, configurations, and architectures. Here are some common types of VPNs:

1. Site-to-Site VPNs

Type: Hardware-based VPNs

Function: Establish secure and encrypted connections between two or more geographically distributed networks, such as branch offices, data centers, and cloud environments, to facilitate seamless communication, data sharing, and resource access across locations.

2. Remote Access VPNs

Type: Software-based VPNs

Function: Enable remote users, employees, and partners to securely access and connect to internal networks, resources, and applications from remote locations using VPN clients, applications, and mobile devices, ensuring secure and private remote access and connectivity.

3. SSL/TLS VPNs

Type: Web-based VPNs

Function: Utilize SSL/TLS encryption protocols and web browsers to establish secure and encrypted connections between users' devices and internal networks, enabling secure remote access to web-based applications, services, and resources without requiring dedicated VPN clients or software.

Benefits of VPNs

Implementing VPNs offers various benefits and advantages for organizations and individuals looking to enhance their network security, privacy, and accessibility. Here are some key benefits of VPNs:

1. Enhanced Security and Privacy

Benefit: Protect sensitive data, communications, and online activities from unauthorized access, interception, and surveillance by encrypting and securing connections between users' devices and VPN servers.

2. Secure Remote Access

Benefit: Enable secure and private remote access to internal networks, resources, and applications for remote users, employees, and partners from anywhere, facilitating flexible and remote work environments without compromising security.

3. Geo-restriction Bypassing

Benefit: Bypass geographic restrictions, content limitations, and censorship by masking users' IP addresses and routing traffic through VPN servers located in different regions, allowing access to restricted content, services, and websites from anywhere in the world.

Best Practices for VPNs

Implementing best practices for VPNs is essential for maximizing security, performance, and reliability while minimizing risks, vulnerabilities, and potential issues. Here are some recommended best practices for VPNs:

1. Strong Encryption and Authentication

Implement: Utilize strong encryption algorithms, protocols, and authentication methods, such as AES-256, SHA-256, and RSA, to ensure robust encryption, data protection, and secure authentication for VPN connections and communications.

2. Regular Updates and Patch Management

Implement: Keep VPN servers, clients, and software up-to-date with the latest security patches, updates, and fixes provided by vendors to address known vulnerabilities, and security weaknesses, and protect against exploits and malware.

3. Multi-factor Authentication (MFA)

Implement: Enable multi-factor authentication (MFA) for VPN access, requiring additional verification and authentication steps, such as one-time passwords (OTP), biometric verification, and smart cards, to enhance user account security and prevent unauthorized access.

Virtual Private Networks (VPNs) play a crucial role in modern network security infrastructure, providing secure, private, and reliable connections over public networks to protect data transmission, communication, and remote access effectively. By understanding the concepts, functionalities, types, benefits, and best practices of VPNs, organizations, and individuals can implement robust VPN solutions, strategies, and controls to safeguard network resources, services, and data against evolving cyber threats, attacks, and vulnerabilities.

As we continue to explore the dynamic and challenging landscape of cybersecurity in the following chapters, we will delve deeper into advanced techniques, tools, and strategies for securing systems, networks, and applications and defending against evolving cyber threats and attack vectors.

8.3 Secure Network Design and Configuration

Secure network design and configuration are essential components of robust network security strategies, focusing on creating and maintaining a secure, resilient, and reliable network infrastructure that safeguards data, applications, and resources from unauthorized access, malicious activities, and potential threats. Proper network design and configuration involve implementing security principles, best practices and controls to mitigate risks, vulnerabilities, and exposures, ensuring confidentiality, integrity, and availability across the network. In this section, we'll explore the concepts, principles, methodologies, and best practices of secure network design and configuration to help you build and maintain a secure and effective network environment.

Principles of Secure Network Design

Secure network design principles guide the development and implementation of network architectures, configurations, and policies to ensure a strong security posture and defense-in-depth strategy. Here are some fundamental principles of secure network design:

1. Least Privilege and Access Control

Principle: Implement least privilege access controls, restricting and limiting user permissions, privileges, and access rights based on roles, responsibilities, and requirements to minimize the potential impact of unauthorized access and privilege escalation.

2. Defense-in-Depth

Principle: Adopt a layered security approach, combining multiple security controls, technologies, and measures, such as firewalls, IDS/IPS, encryption, and monitoring, to create multiple lines of defense and protect against a wide range of cyber threats and attack vectors.

3. Segmentation and Isolation

Principle: Segment and isolate network resources, devices, and services into separate network zones and segments, implementing network segmentation, VLANs, and DMZs to contain and control the spread of potential compromises, breaches, and lateral movement within the network.

4. Redundancy and High Availability

Principle: Design and implement redundant and fault-tolerant network architectures, components, and configurations, utilizing failover, load balancing, and clustering techniques to ensure continuous operation, availability, and resilience against failures, disruptions, and outages.

Best Practices for Secure Network Configuration

Implementing best practices for secure network configuration is crucial for maintaining a strong security posture, and minimizing risks, vulnerabilities, and exposures while optimizing network performance, reliability, and efficiency. Here are some recommended best practices for secure network configuration:

1. Secure Configuration Baselines

Implement: Establish and maintain secure configuration baselines and standards for network devices, systems, and applications, following industry guidelines, vendor recommendations, and security best practices to ensure consistent and secure configurations across the network.

2. Regular Security Audits and Assessments

Implement: Conduct regular security audits, assessments, and reviews of network configurations, policies, and controls using automated scanning tools, manual inspections, and penetration testing to identify, assess, and remediate security weaknesses, misconfigurations, and vulnerabilities proactively.

3. Network Monitoring and Logging

Implement: Deploy network monitoring tools, logging solutions, and SIEM platforms to continuously monitor, analyze, and record network activities, events, and behaviors, generating alerts, notifications, and reports on suspicious activities, potential security incidents, and compliance violations for timely detection, response, and investigation.

4. Patch Management and Firmware Updates

Implement: Establish a proactive patch management and firmware update process for network devices, systems, and appliances, regularly applying security patches, updates, and fixes provided by vendors to address known vulnerabilities, and security weaknesses, and protect against exploits, malware, and cyber threats.

Secure network design and configuration are fundamental aspects of network security, emphasizing the importance of implementing robust security principles, best practices, and controls to create and maintain a secure, resilient, and reliable network environment. By understanding the principles of secure network design, adopting best practices for secure network configuration, and continuously monitoring, assessing, and improving network security, organizations and individuals can build and maintain a strong security posture, protect network resources and data, and defend against evolving cyber threats, attacks, and vulnerabilities effectively.

As we continue to explore the dynamic and challenging landscape of cybersecurity in the following chapters, we will delve deeper into advanced techniques, tools, and strategies for securing systems, networks, and applications and defending against evolving cyber threats and attack vectors.

Chapter 9: Incident Response and Forensics

Incident response and forensics are critical components of cybersecurity that focus on preparing for, responding to, and investigating security incidents, breaches, and violations to mitigate risks, minimize impacts, and facilitate recovery and remediation efforts effectively. Incident response involves establishing and implementing strategies, procedures, and processes to detect, analyze, and respond to security incidents and breaches in a timely and coordinated manner. Forensics, on the other hand, involves collecting, analyzing, and preserving digital evidence and artifacts to identify, investigate, and attribute security incidents, breaches, and cybercrimes. In this chapter, we'll explore the concepts, methodologies, best practices, and tools of incident response and forensics to help you understand their significance and application in cybersecurity.

1. Incident Response

Incident response is a structured approach and process for managing and handling security incidents, breaches, and violations to ensure effective detection, analysis, containment, eradication, recovery, and communication of incidents and their impacts. A well-defined incident response plan (IRP) enables organizations to respond promptly and efficiently to security incidents, minimize damage, and restore normal operations with minimal disruptions. Here are the key stages and components of incident response:

- **Preparation**

Stage: Develop and implement incident response policies, procedures, and plans, including incident detection and reporting mechanisms, communication strategies, roles and responsibilities, and resources and tools required for effective incident response and management.

- **Detection and Analysis**

Stage: Monitor and detect security incidents and anomalies using security monitoring tools, intrusion detection systems (IDS), and security information and event management (SIEM) platforms, analyze and investigate detected incidents to assess their nature, scope, and impact accurately.

- **Containment, Eradication, and Recovery**

Stage: Implement containment strategies and measures to prevent the spread and escalation of incidents, eradicate and remove malicious activities and threats from affected systems, and restore and recover impacted services, applications, and data to normal operations.

- **Post-Incident Analysis and Lessons Learned**

Stage: Conduct post-incident analysis, review, and evaluation of incident response activities, identify lessons learned, gaps, and areas for improvement, and update and refine incident response plans, processes, and strategies based on insights, experiences, and feedback from incidents.

2. Forensics

Forensics is the science and practice of collecting, analyzing, and preserving digital evidence and artifacts from computer systems, networks, and storage devices to investigate, identify, and attribute security incidents, breaches, cybercrimes, and malicious activities. Digital forensics plays a crucial role in incident response, legal proceedings, and cybersecurity investigations, providing insights, evidence, and intelligence to support investigations, prosecutions, and remediation efforts. Here are the key stages and components of digital forensics:

- **Evidence Collection**

Stage: Collect and gather digital evidence and artifacts from computers, servers, networks, and storage devices using forensically sound and approved methods, tools, and procedures to preserve the integrity, authenticity, and chain of custody of evidence.

- **Evidence Analysis and Examination**

Stage: Analyze and examine collected digital evidence using forensic analysis tools, techniques, and methodologies to uncover, extract, and interpret relevant information, data, and activities related to security incidents, breaches, and cybercrimes.

- **Reporting and Documentation**

Stage: Document and report forensic findings, observations, and conclusions in comprehensive and detailed forensic reports, providing clear and concise explanations, analyses, and evidence to support investigations, legal proceedings, and remediation efforts effectively.

- **Legal Proceedings and Testimony**

Stage: Collaborate and cooperate with legal authorities, law enforcement agencies, and legal teams to support investigations, prosecutions, and court proceedings, providing expert testimony, evidence, and insights to assist in identifying, prosecuting, and convicting perpetrators and offenders of cybercrimes and malicious activities.

Incident response and forensics are essential disciplines in cybersecurity, focusing on preparing for, responding to, and investigating security incidents, breaches, and cybercrimes to protect organizations and individuals from risks, threats, and vulnerabilities effectively. By understanding the concepts, methodologies, best practices, and tools of incident response and forensics, organizations and individuals can develop and implement robust incident response and forensics capabilities, strategies, and processes to enhance their cybersecurity posture, resilience, and readiness to detect, respond to, and recover from security incidents and breaches proactively.

As we continue to explore the dynamic and challenging landscape of cybersecurity in the following chapters, we will delve deeper into advanced techniques, tools, and strategies for securing systems, networks, and applications and defending against evolving cyber threats and attack vectors.

9.1 Incident Response Process

The incident response process is a structured and systematic approach to managing and handling security incidents, breaches, and violations effectively to minimize damage, mitigate risks, and facilitate recovery and remediation efforts. An effective incident response process enables organizations to detect, analyze, contain, eradicate, and recover from security incidents in a timely and coordinated manner, ensuring the confidentiality, integrity, and availability of data, systems, and services. In this section, we'll delve into the key stages, components, and best practices of the incident response process to provide you with a comprehensive understanding of its importance and implementation in cybersecurity.

Key Stages of the Incident Response Process

The incident response process consists of several key stages that guide the identification, assessment, containment, eradication, recovery, and communication of security incidents and their impacts. Here are the primary stages of the incident response process:

1. Preparation

Stage Objective: Develop, implement, and maintain incident response policies, procedures, plans, and resources to prepare and equip the organization with the necessary tools, knowledge, and capabilities to respond effectively to security incidents and breaches.

Activities:

- Establish an incident response team (IRT) with defined roles, responsibilities, and expertise.
- Develop incident response policies, procedures, and plans, including incident detection, reporting, communication, and escalation mechanisms.
- Conduct regular training, drills, and simulations to enhance incident response readiness, awareness, and coordination among team members and stakeholders.
- Implement and maintain incident detection and response tools, technologies, and solutions, such as intrusion detection systems (IDS), security information and event management (SIEM) platforms, and endpoint detection and response (EDR) solutions.

2. Detection and Analysis

Stage Objective: Detect, analyze, and assess security incidents and anomalies to determine their nature, scope, impact, and severity accurately, enabling informed decision-making and response actions.

Activities:

- Monitor and analyze network traffic, logs, and activities using monitoring tools, IDS, SIEM platforms, and EDR solutions to detect and identify security incidents, breaches, and suspicious behaviors.
- Investigate and analyze detected incidents, assessing their nature, characteristics, and potential impacts on systems, networks, data, and services.
- Prioritize and categorize incidents based on their severity, impact, and criticality to focus and allocate resources, efforts, and responses effectively.

3. Containment, Eradication, and Recovery

Stage Objective: Implement containment strategies and measures to prevent the spread and escalation of incidents, eradicate malicious activities and threats from affected systems, and restore and recover impacted services, applications, and data to normal operations.

Activities:

- Isolate and contain affected systems, networks, and resources to prevent the spread and propagation of incidents and mitigate further risks and damages.
- Eradicate and remove malicious activities, threats, and vulnerabilities from affected systems, networks, and environments using remediation and mitigation techniques, tools, and solutions.

- Restore and recover impacted services, applications, and data to normal operations, ensuring availability, functionality, and performance while maintaining security and integrity.

4. Post-Incident Analysis and Lessons Learned

Stage Objective: Conduct post-incident analysis, review, and evaluation of incident response activities, outcomes, and experiences to identify lessons learned, gaps, and areas for improvement, and refine incident response plans, processes, and strategies accordingly.

Activities:

- Analyze and evaluate incident response activities, actions, and outcomes to assess effectiveness, efficiency, and performance in managing and handling security incidents and breaches.
- Identify and document lessons learned, challenges, successes, and insights from incidents to improve incident response capabilities, strategies, and processes proactively.
- Update, refine, and enhance incident response plans, procedures, policies, and resources based on post-incident analysis, feedback, and recommendations to optimize incident response readiness, resilience, and effectiveness.

The incident response process is a critical component of cybersecurity, providing organizations with a structured and systematic approach to managing and handling security incidents, breaches, and violations effectively. By understanding and implementing the key stages, components, and best practices of the incident response process, organizations can develop and maintain robust incident response capabilities, strategies, and processes to enhance their cybersecurity posture, resilience, and readiness to detect, respond to, and recover from security incidents and breaches proactively.

As we continue to explore the dynamic and challenging landscape of cybersecurity in the following chapters, we will delve deeper into advanced techniques, tools, and strategies for securing systems, networks, and applications and defending against evolving cyber threats and attack vectors.

9.2 Digital Forensics Fundamentals

Digital forensics is a specialized discipline within cybersecurity that focuses on the collection, preservation, analysis, and presentation of digital evidence and artifacts from computer systems, networks, and storage devices to investigate, identify, and attribute security incidents, breaches, cybercrimes, and malicious activities. Digital forensics plays a crucial role in incident response, legal proceedings, and cybersecurity investigations, providing valuable insights, evidence, and intelligence to support investigations, prosecutions, and remediation efforts effectively. In this section, we'll explore the concepts, methodologies, tools, and best practices of digital forensics to provide you with a comprehensive understanding of its importance and application in cybersecurity.

Key Concepts of Digital Forensics

Digital forensics encompasses various key concepts, principles, and methodologies that guide the collection, analysis, and interpretation of digital evidence and artifacts in cybersecurity investigations. Here are some fundamental concepts of digital forensics:

1. Digital Evidence

Concept: Digital evidence refers to the data, information, and artifacts extracted, collected, and analyzed from computer systems, networks, and storage devices, including files, logs, emails, messages, metadata, and configurations, that provide insights, traces, and proofs of security incidents, breaches, and cybercrimes.

2. Forensic Imaging and Preservation

Concept: Forensic imaging involves creating exact, bit-by-bit copies or images of digital storage media, such as hard drives, SSDs, and memory cards, using forensically sound and approved methods and tools to preserve the integrity, authenticity, and chain of custody of digital evidence and artifacts during investigations.

3. Data Acquisition and Extraction

Concept: Data acquisition and extraction involve retrieving and extracting digital evidence and artifacts from computer systems, networks, and storage devices using specialized forensic tools, techniques, and procedures, ensuring the preservation, integrity, and authenticity of collected data for analysis and investigation.

4. Forensic Analysis and Examination

Concept: Forensic analysis and examination focus on analyzing, examining, and interpreting collected digital evidence and artifacts using forensic analysis tools, methodologies, and techniques to uncover, extract, and interpret relevant information, activities, and events related to security incidents, breaches, and cybercrimes.

5. Reporting and Documentation

Concept: Reporting and documentation involve documenting and reporting forensic findings, observations, and conclusions in comprehensive and detailed forensic reports, providing clear and concise explanations, analyses, and evidence to support investigations, legal proceedings, and remediation efforts effectively.

Digital Forensics Process and Methodologies

The digital forensics process consists of several stages and methodologies that guide the systematic and structured collection, analysis, and interpretation of digital evidence and artifacts in cybersecurity investigations. Here are the primary stages of the digital forensics process:

1. Identification

Stage Objective: Identify and locate potential sources of digital evidence and artifacts from computer systems, networks, and storage devices, including devices, files, logs, and configurations, relevant to the investigation and analysis of security incidents, breaches, and cybercrimes.

2. Preservation

Stage Objective: Preserve and protect digital evidence and artifacts by creating forensic images and maintaining the integrity, authenticity, and chain of custody of collected data, ensuring its admissibility, reliability, and usability in investigations, prosecutions, and legal proceedings.

3. Collection

Stage Objective: Collect and retrieve digital evidence and artifacts from computer systems, networks, and storage devices using forensically sound and approved methods, tools, and procedures, ensuring the preservation, completeness, and integrity of collected data for analysis and examination.

4. Analysis

Stage Objective: Analyze, examine, and interpret collected digital evidence and artifacts using forensic analysis tools, techniques, and methodologies to uncover, extract, and interpret relevant information, activities, and events related to security incidents, breaches, and cybercrimes.

5. Reporting

Stage Objective: Document and report forensic findings, observations, and conclusions in comprehensive and detailed forensic reports, providing clear and concise explanations, analyses, and evidence to support investigations, legal proceedings, and remediation efforts effectively.

Digital forensics is a critical discipline in cybersecurity, providing organizations and investigators with the tools, techniques, and methodologies to collect, preserve, analyze, and present digital evidence and artifacts from computer systems, networks, and storage devices in investigations, legal proceedings, and cybersecurity incidents. By understanding the concepts, methodologies, tools, and best practices of digital forensics, organizations, and individuals can develop and maintain robust digital forensics capabilities, strategies, and processes to enhance their cybersecurity posture, resilience, and readiness to investigate, identify, and respond to security incidents, breaches, and cybercrimes effectively.

As we continue to explore the dynamic and challenging landscape of cybersecurity in the following chapters, we will delve deeper into advanced techniques, tools, and strategies for securing systems, networks, and applications and defending against evolving cyber threats and attack vectors.

9.3 Tools and Techniques for Digital Forensics

Digital forensics relies heavily on specialized tools and techniques designed to collect, preserve, analyze, and interpret digital evidence and artifacts from computer systems, networks, and storage devices. These tools and techniques play a vital role in conducting effective and efficient digital investigations, identifying security incidents, breaches, cybercrimes, and malicious activities, and supporting legal proceedings and remediation efforts. In this section, we'll explore some of the essential tools and techniques used in digital forensics to provide you with insights into their functionalities, capabilities, and applications in cybersecurity investigations.

Essential Digital Forensics Tools

Various digital forensics tools are available, each designed to perform specific tasks and functions in the collection, preservation, analysis, and reporting of digital evidence and artifacts. Here are some essential digital forensics tools commonly used in cybersecurity investigations:

1. Forensic Imaging Tools

- **Tools**: FTK Imager, dd (disk dump), EnCase Forensic, WinHex
- **Function**: Create exact, bit-by-bit copies or images of digital storage media to preserve the integrity, authenticity, and chain of custody of digital evidence and artifacts during investigations.

2. Data Acquisition and Extraction Tools

- **Tools**: Magnet AXIOM, Oxygen Forensic Detective, X-Ways Forensics
- **Function**: Retrieve and extract digital evidence and artifacts from computer systems, networks, and storage devices using specialized forensic tools and techniques to collect, preserve, and analyze data for investigations.

3. Forensic Analysis and Examination Tools

- **Tools**: Autopsy, Sleuth Kit, Volatility, Cellebrite UFED
- **Function**: Analyze, examine, and interpret collected digital evidence and artifacts using forensic analysis tools and techniques to uncover, extract, and interpret relevant information, activities, and events related to security incidents, breaches, and cybercrimes.

4. Memory Forensics Tools

- **Tools**: Rekall, LiME, DumpIt, WinDbg
- **Function**: Analyze and examine volatile memory (RAM) data and processes to uncover and extract valuable information, artifacts, and evidence related to running applications, processes, and activities during investigations.

5. Network Forensics Tools

- **Tools**: Wireshark, tcpdump, NetworkMiner, NetworkForensicsToolkit
- **Function**: Monitor, capture, and analyze network traffic and communications to identify, investigate, and trace security incidents, breaches, and suspicious activities across networks, systems, and devices.

Digital Forensics Techniques and Methodologies

Digital forensics techniques and methodologies guide the systematic and structured collection, analysis, and interpretation of digital evidence and artifacts in cybersecurity investigations. Here are some essential digital forensics techniques commonly used in digital investigations:

1. File System Analysis

Technique: Analyze and examine file systems, directories, and structures to identify, extract, and interpret files, documents, logs, and configurations related to security incidents, breaches, and cybercrimes.

2. Keyword Search and String Matching

Technique: Perform keyword searches, string matching, and regular expressions analysis on digital evidence and artifacts to identify and extract relevant information, data, and patterns related to security incidents, breaches, and cybercrimes.

3. Timeline Analysis

Technique: Create and analyze timelines of digital evidence and artifacts to reconstruct sequences of events, activities, and actions related to security incidents, breaches, and cybercrimes and identify anomalies, discrepancies, and suspicious activities.

4. Hash Analysis and Integrity Verification

Technique: Calculate and compare file hashes (MD5, SHA-1, SHA-256) of digital evidence and artifacts to verify the integrity, authenticity, and consistency of data and detect modifications, alterations, and tampering during investigations.

5. Metadata Analysis

Technique: Examine and analyze metadata (timestamps, file attributes, authorship, and location) of digital evidence and artifacts to gather additional information, context, and insights related to security incidents, breaches, and cybercrimes.

Digital forensics tools and techniques are essential components of cybersecurity investigations, providing organizations and investigators with the capabilities to collect, preserve, analyze, and interpret digital evidence and artifacts effectively and efficiently. By leveraging the power of specialized digital forensics tools and techniques, organizations and individuals can conduct thorough investigations, identify and attribute security incidents, breaches, and cybercrimes, and support legal proceedings and remediation efforts with robust evidence and insights.

As we continue to explore the dynamic and challenging landscape of cybersecurity in the following chapters, we will delve deeper into advanced techniques, strategies, and best practices for securing systems, networks, and applications, and defending against evolving cyber threats and attack vectors.

Chapter 10: Legal and Ethical Considerations

Navigating the complex landscape of cybersecurity involves not only technical proficiency but also a thorough understanding of the legal and ethical frameworks governing the use, management, and protection of information, systems, and networks. As cyber threats continue to evolve and cybercrimes become more sophisticated, the importance of adhering to legal and ethical principles becomes paramount in maintaining trust, integrity, and compliance in the digital realm. In this chapter, we'll explore the legal and ethical considerations that cybersecurity professionals, organizations, and individuals must be aware of to ensure responsible and lawful practices in cybersecurity operations, investigations, and engagements.

Legal Considerations in Cybersecurity

Understanding the legal aspects of cybersecurity is essential for ensuring compliance with applicable laws, regulations, and standards that govern the protection, privacy, and security of information, systems, and networks. Here are some key legal considerations in cybersecurity:

1. Data Protection and Privacy Laws

Laws: GDPR, CCPA, HIPAA, PIPEDA

Considerations: Understand and comply with data protection and privacy laws that regulate the collection, processing, storage, and sharing of personal and sensitive data, ensuring the confidentiality, integrity, and availability of data and respecting individuals' rights and freedoms.

2. Cybercrime Laws and Regulations

- **Laws**: Computer Fraud and Abuse Act (CFAA), Cybersecurity Information Sharing Act (CISA), Computer Misuse Act
- **Considerations**: Familiarize yourself with cybercrime laws and regulations that define and prohibit unauthorized access, hacking, fraud, identity theft, and other illegal activities related to computer systems, networks, and digital data, and adhere to legal requirements and consequences.

3. Intellectual Property Rights and Regulations

- **Laws**: Copyright Act, Digital Millennium Copyright Act (DMCA), Patent Law
- **Considerations**: Respect and protect intellectual property rights and regulations that govern the creation, use, distribution, and protection of copyrighted materials, software, inventions, and proprietary information, ensuring compliance with legal requirements and ethical standards.

4. Incident Reporting and Notification Requirements

- **Laws**: State Data Breach Notification Laws, GDPR Article 33 and 34

- **Considerations**: Be aware of incident reporting and notification requirements that mandate organizations to report security incidents, breaches, and data breaches to regulatory authorities, affected individuals, and stakeholders within specified timelines and comply with legal obligations and responsibilities.

Ethical Considerations in Cybersecurity

Maintaining ethical standards and principles is crucial for fostering trust, integrity, and accountability in cybersecurity practices, operations, and engagements. Here are some key ethical considerations in cybersecurity:

1. Professional Responsibility and Integrity

Principles: Uphold professional responsibility, integrity, and honesty in all cybersecurity activities, engagements, and interactions, demonstrating ethical behavior, transparency, and accountability in decision-making and actions.

2. Respect for Privacy and Confidentiality

Principles: Respect and protect individuals' privacy, confidentiality, and personal data by implementing appropriate safeguards, controls, and measures to prevent unauthorized access, disclosure, and misuse of sensitive information and ensure compliance with privacy laws and regulations.

3. Transparency and Accountability

Principles: Maintain transparency, openness, and accountability in cybersecurity practices, operations, and communications by providing clear, honest, and accurate information, disclosures, and notifications to stakeholders, customers, and the public about security incidents, breaches, and data breaches.

4. Continuous Learning and Improvement

Principles: Foster a culture of continuous learning, growth, and improvement in cybersecurity knowledge, skills, and practices by staying updated with the latest trends, technologies, threats, and best practices, and engaging in professional development, training, and certifications to enhance cybersecurity capabilities, effectiveness, and readiness.

Legal and ethical considerations are integral components of cybersecurity, shaping the practices, principles, and behaviors of professionals, organizations, and individuals in the digital age. By understanding and adhering to the legal and ethical frameworks governing cybersecurity, we can foster responsible, lawful, and ethical practices, protect individuals' rights and freedoms, ensure compliance with legal requirements and standards, and build trust, credibility, and resilience in cybersecurity operations, engagements, and relationships.

As we continue to explore the dynamic and challenging landscape of cybersecurity in the following chapters, we will delve deeper into advanced techniques, strategies, and best practices for securing systems, networks, and applications, and defending against evolving cyber threats and attack vectors while maintaining legal and ethical compliance and integrity.

10.1 Laws and Regulations in Cybersecurity

In the ever-evolving landscape of cybersecurity, laws and regulations play a pivotal role in shaping the practices, responsibilities, and obligations of organizations, professionals, and individuals. These legal frameworks aim to safeguard information, systems, and networks, protect individuals' rights and freedoms, and ensure accountability, transparency, and compliance in cybersecurity operations, engagements, and interactions. In this section, we'll explore some of the prominent laws and regulations governing cybersecurity at the national and international levels, highlighting their key provisions, implications, and impact on cybersecurity practices and responsibilities.

Major Cybersecurity Laws and Regulations

1. General Data Protection Regulation (GDPR)

Jurisdiction: European Union (EU)

- **Purpose**: Protect individuals' personal data and privacy rights by regulating the collection, processing, storage, and sharing of personal and sensitive data by organizations.
- **Key Provisions**: Consent, Data Protection Impact Assessments (DPIA), Data Breach Notifications, Right to Access, Right to

Erasure (Right to be Forgotten), Data Portability, Accountability, and Fines for Non-compliance.

- **Implications**: Organizations must implement robust data protection measures, privacy policies, and compliance frameworks to safeguard personal data and ensure GDPR compliance, with potential severe fines and penalties for non-compliance.

2. California Consumer Privacy Act (CCPA)

- **Jurisdiction**: California, United States
- **Purpose**: Enhance consumer privacy rights and protections by regulating the collection, processing, sale, and sharing of personal information by businesses.
- **Key Provisions**: Consumer Rights (Right to Know, Right to Delete), Opt-out Rights, Data Protection Assessments, Data Breach Notifications, and Non-discrimination.
- **Implications**: Businesses must implement comprehensive data protection and privacy practices, policies, and procedures to comply with CCPA requirements, with potential fines and liabilities for violations and breaches of consumer privacy rights.

3. Health Insurance Portability and Accountability Act (HIPAA)

Jurisdiction: United States (U.S.)

- **Purpose**: Protect individuals' health information privacy and security by regulating the use, disclosure, and safeguarding of

Protected Health Information (PHI) by covered entities and business associates.

- **Key Provisions**: Privacy Rule, Security Rule, Breach Notification Rule, Individual Rights, and Enforcement.
- **Implications**: Covered entities and business associates must implement HIPAA-compliant policies, procedures, and safeguards to protect PHI and ensure compliance with HIPAA requirements, with potential penalties and sanctions for non-compliance and breaches.

4. Computer Fraud and Abuse Act (CFAA)

Jurisdiction: United States (U.S.)

- **Purpose**: Combat computer-related crimes, unauthorized access, hacking, fraud, and misuse of computer systems, networks, and data.
- **Key Provisions**: Unauthorized Access, Unauthorized Exceeding Authorized Access, Fraud, Trafficking in Passwords, and Damaging Protected Computers.
- **Implications**: Individuals and entities must refrain from engaging in unauthorized access, hacking, fraud, and malicious activities targeting computer systems, networks, and data, with potential criminal and civil liabilities, penalties, and prosecutions under the CFAA.

Laws and regulations in cybersecurity form the legal foundations and frameworks governing the protection, privacy, security, and integrity of information, systems, and networks in the digital age. By understanding and adhering to these legal frameworks, organizations, professionals, and individuals can foster responsible, lawful, and ethical practices, safeguard individuals' rights and freedoms, ensure compliance with legal requirements and standards, and mitigate risks, liabilities, and consequences associated with non-compliance, violations, and breaches.

As we continue to explore the dynamic and challenging landscape of cybersecurity in the following chapters, we will delve deeper into advanced techniques, strategies, and best practices for securing systems, networks, and applications, and defending against evolving cyber threats and attack vectors while maintaining legal and ethical compliance and integrity.

10.2 Ethical Guidelines for Ethical Hackers

Ethical hacking, also known as penetration testing or white hat hacking, involves authorized and legitimate efforts to identify, assess, and exploit vulnerabilities in computer systems, networks, and applications to uncover weaknesses, enhance security, and mitigate risks and threats. Ethical hackers play a vital role in cybersecurity by helping organizations identify and address security vulnerabilities proactively, enhancing their resilience and readiness against cyber threats and attacks. However, ethical hacking comes with significant responsibilities and ethical considerations to ensure lawful, responsible, and ethical practices in hacking activities and engagements. In this section, we'll explore the ethical guidelines and principles that ethical hackers must adhere to maintain integrity, trustworthiness, and professionalism in their hacking endeavors.

Ethical Guidelines for Ethical Hackers

1. Authorization and Permission

- **Guideline**: Obtain explicit authorization and permission from the organization or individual before conducting any hacking activities, penetration testing, or vulnerability assessments on their systems, networks, or applications.
- **Rationale**: Ensure lawful and authorized hacking engagements, prevent unauthorized access, breaches, and legal repercussions, and establish trust, transparency, and accountability with stakeholders and clients.

2. Scope and Limitations

- **Guideline**: Define and adhere to the scope, objectives, limitations, and boundaries of the hacking engagement, including target systems, networks, applications, and permissible activities, to avoid unintended consequences, disruptions, and damages.
- **Rationale**: Focus hacking efforts, resources, and actions on authorized and targeted areas, prevent collateral damage, disruptions, and unintended consequences, and maintain alignment with client expectations, requirements, and goals.

3. Confidentiality and Non-disclosure

- **Guideline**: Maintain strict confidentiality, secrecy, and non-disclosure of sensitive information, data, findings, vulnerabilities, exploits, and penetration testing results obtained during hacking engagements to protect clients' privacy, security, and interests.

- **Rationale**: Safeguard clients' confidential and proprietary information, data, and assets from unauthorized access, disclosure, misuse, and exploitation, and maintain trust, privacy, and confidentiality in hacking activities and communications.

4. Integrity and Professionalism

- **Guideline**: Uphold high standards of integrity, professionalism, and ethical conduct in all hacking activities, engagements, and interactions by demonstrating honesty, transparency, respect, and responsibility in decision-making, actions, and communications.
- **Rationale**: Foster trust, credibility, and reputation as a trustworthy, reliable, and ethical hacker, establish positive and constructive relationships with clients, stakeholders, and the cybersecurity community, and promote ethical hacking practices, principles, and values.

5. Compliance and Accountability

- **Guideline**: Comply with applicable laws, regulations, standards, and ethical guidelines governing hacking, cybersecurity, and privacy, and take responsibility and accountability for hacking activities, findings, actions, and outcomes to mitigate risks, liabilities, and consequences.
- **Rationale**: Ensure lawful, responsible, and accountable hacking engagements, avoid legal repercussions, penalties, and sanctions, and demonstrate commitment, diligence, and adherence to legal

and ethical compliance in hacking operations, practices, and engagements.

Ethical hacking is a valuable and essential practice in cybersecurity, enabling organizations to identify, assess, and address security vulnerabilities proactively and enhance their resilience and readiness against cyber threats and attacks. By adhering to ethical guidelines and principles, ethical hackers can conduct lawful, responsible, and ethical hacking engagements, maintain integrity, trustworthiness, and professionalism, and contribute positively and constructively to cybersecurity efforts, initiatives, and advancements.

As we continue to explore the dynamic and challenging landscape of cybersecurity in the following chapters, we will delve deeper into advanced techniques, strategies, and best practices for securing systems, networks, and applications, and defending against evolving cyber threats and attack vectors while maintaining legal and ethical compliance, integrity, and professionalism.

10.3 Reporting Security Vulnerabilities Responsibly

In the ever-evolving landscape of cybersecurity, the discovery and disclosure of security vulnerabilities play a crucial role in enhancing the security, resilience, and readiness of systems, networks, and applications against cyber threats and attacks. Responsible vulnerability disclosure involves identifying, assessing, and reporting security vulnerabilities to the affected organizations, vendors, or developers in a timely, transparent, and collaborative manner to facilitate prompt remediation, mitigation, and resolution of vulnerabilities and protect users, organizations, and assets from potential risks and threats. In this section, we'll explore the principles, best practices, and guidelines for reporting security vulnerabilities responsibly and effectively to foster a safer and more secure digital ecosystem.

Principles of Responsible Vulnerability Disclosure

1. Authorization and Permission

- **Principle**: Obtain explicit authorization and permission from the affected organization, vendor, or developer before conducting vulnerability assessments, testing, or disclosing vulnerabilities to ensure lawful, authorized, and collaborative engagement and communication.
- **Rationale**: Establish trust, transparency, and cooperation with the organization, vendor, or developer, prevent unauthorized access, breaches, and legal repercussions, and facilitate responsible and effective vulnerability disclosure and remediation.

2. Timeliness and Transparency

- **Principle**: Report security vulnerabilities to the affected organization, vendor, or developer promptly and openly, providing clear, detailed, and accurate information, data, and evidence about the vulnerability, its impact, and potential risks to enable timely and informed decision-making and action.
- **Rationale**: Enable quick identification, assessment, and remediation of vulnerabilities, minimize exposure, exploitation, and damages, and foster open, transparent, and collaborative

communication, cooperation, and coordination between researchers, organizations, and stakeholders.

3. Confidentiality and Non-disclosure

- **Principle**: Maintain confidentiality, secrecy, and non-disclosure of sensitive information, data, findings, vulnerabilities, exploits, and vulnerability reports during the vulnerability disclosure process to protect organizations' privacy, security, and interests and mitigate risks and threats.
- **Rationale**: Safeguard organizations' confidential and proprietary information, data, and assets from unauthorized access, disclosure, misuse, and exploitation, and ensure trust, privacy, and confidentiality in vulnerability disclosure activities and communications.

4. Collaboration and Cooperation

- **Principle**: Collaborate and cooperate with the affected organization, vendor, or developer throughout the vulnerability disclosure process, including verification, validation, remediation, and resolution of vulnerabilities, to facilitate effective, efficient, and constructive engagement and outcomes.
- **Rationale**: Foster positive, productive, and constructive relationships, interactions, and partnerships between researchers, organizations, and stakeholders, promote collaboration, cooperation, and coordination in vulnerability management and response, and enhance the effectiveness, responsiveness, and resilience of cybersecurity efforts and initiatives.

5. Respect and Professionalism

- **Principle**: Show respect, professionalism, and ethical conduct in all vulnerability disclosure activities, engagements, and interactions by demonstrating courtesy, patience, understanding, and empathy toward organizations, vendors, developers, and stakeholders involved in the vulnerability management and response process.
- **Rationale**: Build trust, credibility, and reputation as a responsible, respectful, and professional security researcher, establish positive and constructive relationships with organizations, vendors, developers, and stakeholders, and promote ethical, responsible, and respectful vulnerability disclosure practices, principles, and values.

Best Practices for Responsible Vulnerability Disclosure

- **Documentation**: Document all stages, steps, activities, and communications of the vulnerability disclosure process, including discovery, assessment, verification, reporting, remediation, and resolution, to maintain records, evidence, and accountability and facilitate transparency, traceability, and verification.
- **Communication**: Maintain open, clear, and constructive communication, collaboration, and cooperation with organizations, vendors, developers, and stakeholders involved in the vulnerability disclosure process, providing updates, feedback, and support to facilitate understanding, progress, and success.
- **Feedback Loop**: Establish and maintain a feedback loop with organizations, vendors, developers, and stakeholders to exchange information, insights, and lessons learned from the vulnerability disclosure process, promote continuous learning, improvement,

and innovation, and enhance the effectiveness and efficiency of vulnerability management and response efforts.

Responsible vulnerability disclosure is a critical and valuable practice in cybersecurity, enabling security researchers, organizations, vendors, and developers to collaborate and cooperate in identifying, assessing, and addressing security vulnerabilities proactively and effectively. By adhering to the principles, best practices, and guidelines of responsible vulnerability disclosure, we can foster a safer and more secure digital ecosystem, protect users, organizations, and assets from potential risks and threats, and contribute positively and constructively to cybersecurity efforts, initiatives, and advancements.

As we continue to explore the dynamic and challenging landscape of cybersecurity in the following chapters, we will delve deeper into advanced techniques, strategies, and best practices for securing systems, networks, and applications, and defending against evolving cyber threats and attack vectors while maintaining legal and ethical compliance, integrity, and professionalism.

Chapter 11: Future Trends in Ethical Hacking

As the cybersecurity landscape continues to evolve at a rapid pace, driven by technological advancements, emerging threats, and evolving attack vectors, the field of ethical hacking is also experiencing significant transformations and innovations. Ethical hackers are at the forefront of cybersecurity, continually adapting and evolving their skills, techniques, and strategies to identify, assess, and mitigate security vulnerabilities and risks effectively and proactively. In this chapter, we'll explore the future trends shaping the world of ethical hacking, providing insights into the emerging technologies, methodologies, and practices that will define the next generation of ethical hacking and cybersecurity.

Emerging Technologies in Ethical Hacking

1. Artificial Intelligence (AI) and Machine Learning (ML)

Trend: Integration of AI and ML technologies in ethical hacking tools, platforms, and solutions to enhance automation, analysis, prediction, and decision-making capabilities in vulnerability assessment, threat detection, and response.

Implications: Enable more intelligent, adaptive, and efficient ethical hacking operations, reduce manual efforts, errors, and false positives, and improve accuracy, effectiveness, and scalability in identifying and mitigating security vulnerabilities and threats.

2. Quantum Computing

Trend: Development and utilization of quantum computing technologies and algorithms in cryptographic analysis, encryption, and decryption to explore and exploit vulnerabilities in quantum-resistant and legacy cryptographic systems and protocols.

Implications: Unlock new possibilities, opportunities, and challenges in cybersecurity, cryptography, and ethical hacking, require innovative approaches, strategies, and defenses against quantum computing-enabled attacks, and reshape the future of secure communications and information protection.

3. Internet of Things (IoT) Security

Trend: Focus on IoT security, vulnerabilities, and threats arising from the proliferation of connected devices, sensors, and systems in smart homes, cities, industries, and infrastructures, and the integration of IoT security in ethical hacking practices, methodologies, and engagements.

Implications: Address unique and complex IoT security challenges, risks, and exposures, enhance IoT device, network, and ecosystem security, and develop specialized tools, techniques, and strategies for identifying, assessing, and mitigating IoT-related vulnerabilities and threats.

4. Cloud Security

Trend: Emphasis on cloud security, architectures, configurations, and services in ethical hacking activities, engagements, and assessments to identify, assess, and remediate cloud-specific vulnerabilities, misconfigurations, and exposures in cloud environments, platforms, and infrastructures.

Implications: Enhance cloud resilience, robustness, and reliability, address cloud security risks, threats, and challenges, and develop cloud-focused ethical hacking tools, techniques, and best practices to ensure secure and compliant cloud computing and operations.

Future Methodologies and Practices in Ethical Hacking

1. Red Team Operations

Methodology: Expansion and evolution of red team operations, exercises, and engagements in organizations, industries, and sectors to simulate and assess real-world cyber-attack scenarios, tactics, techniques, and procedures (TTPs), and enhance defensive strategies, capabilities, and readiness.

Implications: Foster proactive, realistic, and practical cybersecurity testing, training, and readiness, identify and address security gaps, weaknesses, and vulnerabilities, and strengthen organizational resilience, responsiveness, and resilience against sophisticated and advanced cyber threats and attacks.

2. DevSecOps Integration

Methodology: Integration of cybersecurity, ethical hacking, and DevSecOps practices, principles, and tools in software development, deployment, and operations lifecycle to embed security, compliance, and quality into the development process, culture, and mindset.

Implications: Promote a culture of security, collaboration, and continuous improvement, enhance security awareness, education, and training, and facilitate secure, compliant, and resilient software development, delivery, and operations in fast-paced, agile, and dynamic environments.

3. Threat Intelligence and Analytics

Methodology: Adoption and utilization of threat intelligence, analytics, and sharing platforms, solutions, and services to gather, analyze, and share actionable insights, indicators of compromise (IOCs), and threat intelligence data on emerging threats, vulnerabilities, and adversaries.

Implications: Enable proactive, informed, and data-driven decision-making, response, and mitigation strategies, improve situational awareness, visibility, and understanding of the threat landscape, and strengthen defenses, detections, and protections against evolving cyber threats, adversaries, and attack vectors.

The future of ethical hacking is filled with exciting opportunities, challenges, and innovations, driven by emerging technologies, methodologies, and practices that will shape the next generation of cybersecurity. Ethical hackers must embrace continuous learning, adaptation, and evolution to stay ahead of the curve, navigate the complexities and uncertainties of the digital landscape, and contribute positively and constructively to safeguarding and securing the digital world.

As we continue to explore the dynamic and challenging landscape of cybersecurity in the following chapters, we will delve deeper into advanced techniques, strategies, and best practices for securing systems, networks, and applications, and defending against evolving cyber threats and attack vectors while maintaining legal and ethical compliance, integrity, and professionalism.

11.1 Emerging Technologies and Threats

The rapid evolution of technology brings forth new opportunities and challenges in the realm of cybersecurity. Emerging technologies are continuously transforming the digital landscape, introducing innovative capabilities, functionalities, and possibilities that redefine the way we live, work, and connect with the world. However, with these advancements come new vulnerabilities, risks, and threats that require vigilant attention, proactive measures, and adaptive strategies to ensure security, resilience, and trust in the digital ecosystem. In this section, we'll explore the emerging technologies and associated threats that are shaping the future of cybersecurity and ethical hacking.

Artificial Intelligence (AI) and Machine Learning (ML)

Emerging Technology: AI and ML are revolutionizing various sectors, including cybersecurity, by enhancing automation, analytics, prediction, and decision-making capabilities in threat detection, vulnerability assessment, and response.

Associated Threats:

- **Adversarial Attacks**: Exploiting vulnerabilities in AI and ML algorithms to manipulate, deceive, and mislead automated systems, models, and predictions.
- **Data Poisoning**: Injecting malicious data, samples, or inputs into AI and ML models to corrupt, compromise, and undermine their accuracy, reliability, and effectiveness.
- **Model Inversion**: Reverse engineering and extracting sensitive information, insights, or features from AI and ML models through unauthorized access, analysis, and exploitation.

Quantum Computing

Emerging Technology: Quantum computing promises to revolutionize computing, cryptography, and communications by leveraging quantum mechanics principles to perform complex computations, solve intricate problems, and explore new frontiers in science, technology, and innovation.

Associated Threats:

- **Cryptographic Breakthroughs**: Leveraging quantum algorithms and capabilities to break, decrypt, and compromise traditional and legacy cryptographic systems, protocols, and algorithms.
- **Secure Communication Vulnerabilities**: Exploiting vulnerabilities in quantum-resistant and post-quantum cryptographic solutions, implementations, and standards to

intercept, eavesdrop, and tamper with secure communications and data transmissions.

- **Resource and Infrastructure Attacks**: Targeting and disrupting quantum computing infrastructures, resources, and ecosystems through denial-of-service (DoS) attacks, malware, and exploits to undermine and compromise quantum computing capabilities and operations.

Internet of Things (IoT) Security

Emerging Technology: The proliferation of connected devices, sensors, and systems in smart homes, cities, industries, and infrastructures is creating a vast and complex IoT ecosystem that offers unprecedented opportunities and challenges in connectivity, automation, and innovation.

Associated Threats:

- **Device Vulnerabilities**: Exploiting vulnerabilities in IoT devices, firmware, software, and configurations to gain unauthorized access, control, and manipulation of connected devices and systems.
- **Network Exploits**: Launching attacks on IoT networks, protocols, and infrastructures to intercept, manipulate, and disrupt communications, data transmissions, and operations.
- **Data Privacy Risks**: Compromising data privacy, confidentiality, and security by exploiting weaknesses in IoT data storage, processing, sharing, and management practices, policies, and implementations.

Emerging technologies are driving transformative changes and advancements in the digital world, offering unprecedented opportunities for innovation, growth, and progress. However, these advancements also introduce new vulnerabilities, risks, and threats that require continuous monitoring, assessment, and mitigation to ensure security, resilience, and trust in the evolving digital ecosystem. Ethical hackers must stay abreast of the latest technological trends, developments, and threats, and adopt proactive, adaptive, and innovative strategies to identify, assess, and address emerging security challenges effectively and responsibly.

As we continue to explore the dynamic and challenging landscape of cybersecurity in the following chapters, we will delve deeper into advanced techniques, strategies, and best practices for securing systems, networks, and applications, and defending against evolving cyber threats and attack vectors while maintaining legal and ethical compliance, integrity, and professionalism.

11.2 Career Opportunities in Ethical Hacking

The field of ethical hacking is a rapidly expanding and dynamic sector within the broader cybersecurity industry, offering a plethora of exciting and rewarding career opportunities for aspiring professionals, enthusiasts, and experts passionate about cybersecurity, technology, and innovation. Ethical hackers play a vital role in safeguarding organizations, businesses, governments, and individuals from cyber threats, vulnerabilities, and attacks by identifying, assessing, and mitigating security risks and vulnerabilities proactively and responsibly. In this section, we'll explore the diverse and promising career opportunities available in ethical hacking and cybersecurity, highlighting the roles, responsibilities, skills, qualifications, and pathways to success in this exciting and ever-evolving field.

Roles and Responsibilities in Ethical Hacking

1. Ethical Hacker/Penetration Tester

Role: Conducting penetration testing, vulnerability assessments, and ethical hacking engagements to identify, assess, and exploit security vulnerabilities and weaknesses in systems, networks, and applications.

Responsibilities: Performing security assessments, penetration tests, vulnerability scans, and ethical hacking activities; analyzing, reporting, and documenting findings; and recommending and implementing remediation and mitigation measures.

2. Security Analyst/Incident Responder

Role: Monitoring, analyzing, and responding to security incidents, breaches, and threats to detect, investigate, and mitigate security incidents and breaches effectively and efficiently.

Responsibilities: Monitoring security alerts and logs; analyzing and investigating security incidents; coordinating and executing incident response activities; and developing, maintaining, and enhancing incident response procedures, processes, and protocols.

3. Security Consultant/Advisor

Role: Providing expert advice, guidance, and consultancy services on cybersecurity, risk management, compliance, and governance to organizations, businesses, governments, and stakeholders.

Responsibilities: Conducting security assessments and audits; developing and implementing cybersecurity strategies, policies, and programs; advising on security best practices, standards, and regulations; and assisting in compliance, certification, and accreditation efforts.

4. Security Researcher/Threat Intelligence Analyst

Role: Researching, analyzing, and investigating emerging cyber threats, vulnerabilities, exploits, and attack vectors to understand, predict, and counteract evolving cyber threats and adversaries effectively.

Responsibilities: Conducting threat intelligence analysis; researching and identifying new vulnerabilities, exploits, and attack methods; developing and sharing threat intelligence reports, insights, and indicators of compromise (IOCs); and collaborating with the cybersecurity community, researchers, and stakeholders.

Skills and Qualifications in Ethical Hacking

- **Technical Skills**: Proficiency in ethical hacking tools, techniques, methodologies, and practices; knowledge of programming languages, scripting, networking, operating systems, and cybersecurity technologies; and hands-on experience in penetration testing, vulnerability assessment, and security analysis.
- **Soft Skills**: Analytical thinking, problem-solving, communication, collaboration, teamwork, adaptability, attention to detail, ethical judgment, and professionalism.
- **Certifications**: Certified Ethical Hacker (CEH), Offensive Security Certified Professional (OSCP), Certified Information

Systems Security Professional (CISSP), Certified Information Security Manager (CISM), and other relevant certifications in cybersecurity, ethical hacking, and information security.

Career Pathways and Development in Ethical Hacking

- **Entry-Level Positions**: Junior Security Analyst, Security Technician, Entry-Level Penetration Tester, and Junior Ethical Hacker roles for newcomers, graduates, and aspiring professionals to gain foundational knowledge, skills, and experience in ethical hacking and cybersecurity.
- **Mid-Level Positions**: Security Consultant, Security Analyst, Penetration Tester, and Ethical Hacker roles for experienced professionals with advanced skills, expertise, and certifications to lead, manage, and execute cybersecurity projects, engagements, and initiatives.
- **Senior-Level Positions**: Senior Security Consultant, Lead Ethical Hacker, Security Manager, and Chief Information Security Officer (CISO) roles for seasoned professionals with extensive experience, leadership capabilities, and strategic vision to oversee, direct, and shape cybersecurity strategies, programs, and operations at organizational, enterprise, and executive levels.

Ethical hacking offers a diverse, dynamic, and rewarding career path for individuals passionate about cybersecurity, technology, and innovation, with abundant opportunities for growth, development, and advancement in various roles, sectors, and industries. Whether you're a newcomer, graduate, professional, or expert in the field, ethical hacking provides a stimulating, challenging, and fulfilling environment to learn, grow, and excel while making a meaningful and impactful contribution to safeguarding and securing the digital world.

As we continue to explore the fascinating world of cybersecurity in the following chapters, we will delve deeper into advanced techniques, strategies, and best practices for securing systems, networks, and applications, and defending against evolving cyber threats and attack vectors while maintaining legal and ethical compliance, integrity, and professionalism.

11.3 Continuous Learning and Professional Development

In the dynamic and ever-evolving field of ethical hacking and cybersecurity, continuous learning and professional development are crucial for staying ahead of the curve, adapting to emerging technologies, threats, and challenges, and maintaining relevance, proficiency, and excellence in the rapidly changing digital landscape. Ethical hackers and cybersecurity professionals must embrace a lifelong learning mindset, commit to ongoing education, training, and certification, and actively seek opportunities to expand their knowledge, skills, and expertise to thrive and succeed in their careers. In this section, we'll explore the importance of continuous learning and professional development in ethical hacking and cybersecurity and provide insights, strategies, and resources to support and guide professionals in their learning journey and career advancement.

Importance of Continuous Learning and Professional Development

1. Stay Updated with Emerging Technologies and Trends

Technology Evolution: Keep abreast of the latest technological advancements, innovations, and trends shaping the cybersecurity landscape, such as AI, ML, quantum computing, IoT, and cloud computing, to understand, adapt, and leverage new tools, techniques, and strategies effectively.

2. Enhance Skills and Expertise

Skill Development: Continuously develop and refine technical, analytical, problem-solving, communication, collaboration, and leadership skills through hands-on practice, experimentation, and real-world experiences to excel in ethical hacking roles and responsibilities.

3. Adapt to Evolving Threats and Challenges

Threat Awareness: Stay informed and vigilant about evolving cyber threats, vulnerabilities, exploits, attack vectors, and adversaries to anticipate, detect, and mitigate emerging risks and challenges effectively and proactively.

4. Career Growth and Advancement

Career Progression: Pursue advanced certifications, qualifications, and roles; acquire specialized knowledge and expertise; and demonstrate commitment, dedication, and excellence in ethical hacking and cybersecurity to unlock new opportunities, responsibilities, and achievements in your career journey.

Strategies for Continuous Learning and Professional Development

1. Engage in Hands-On Practice and Exploration

Practical Experience: Engage in hands-on practice, experimentation, and exploration with ethical hacking tools, platforms, technologies, and environments to develop, enhance, and refine your technical skills, knowledge, and proficiency effectively.

2. Pursue Formal Education and Training

Educational Opportunities: Enroll in formal education programs, courses, workshops, and training sessions in cybersecurity, ethical hacking, information technology, computer science, and related fields to acquire, expand, and deepen your knowledge, insights, and expertise.

3. Obtain Industry-Recognized Certifications

Certification Pathways: Pursue and obtain industry-recognized certifications, such as CEH, OSCP, CISSP, CISM, and others, to validate your skills, capabilities, and qualifications; enhance your credibility, recognition, and marketability; and demonstrate commitment to professional growth and excellence.

4. Join Professional Associations and Communities

Networking and Collaboration: Join professional associations, organizations, forums, groups, and communities, such as ISACA, (ISC)^2, OWASP, and others, to network, collaborate, and engage with fellow professionals, experts, mentors, and peers; share knowledge, experiences, and insights; and build relationships, connections, and opportunities in the cybersecurity community.

Continuous learning and professional development are essential pillars for success, growth, and excellence in the dynamic and challenging field of ethical hacking and cybersecurity. By embracing a lifelong learning mindset, committing to ongoing education, training, and certification, and actively seeking opportunities to expand, refine, and apply your knowledge, skills, and expertise, you can thrive, excel, and make a meaningful and impactful contribution to safeguarding and securing the digital world.

As we continue to explore the fascinating world of cybersecurity in the following chapters, we will delve deeper into advanced techniques, strategies, and best practices for securing systems, networks, and applications, and defending against evolving cyber threats and attack vectors while maintaining legal and ethical compliance, integrity, and professionalism.

Conclusion

In the digital age, where technology intertwines with every aspect of our lives, cybersecurity has become paramount. As we journeyed through this comprehensive guide on ethical hacking, we've explored the fundamental principles, tools, techniques, and practices that form the bedrock of this dynamic and critical field. Ethical hacking is not just about exploiting vulnerabilities or testing systems; it's about safeguarding our digital world, protecting our information, and ensuring the integrity, availability, and confidentiality of our systems, networks, and data.

Understanding the Basics

We began by laying the groundwork, diving deep into the foundational concepts of computer systems, networks, and cybersecurity. By understanding the basics, we built a solid foundation upon which we could explore more advanced topics, delve into sophisticated techniques, and navigate the intricate landscape of ethical hacking and cybersecurity with confidence and clarity.

Exploring Hacking Tools and Techniques

We then embarked on a fascinating exploration of the diverse and powerful hacking tools and techniques employed by ethical hackers to identify, assess, exploit, and mitigate security vulnerabilities and threats effectively. From reconnaissance and scanning to exploitation and post-exploitation, we dissected each phase of the hacking lifecycle, unraveling the complexities, challenges, and intricacies involved in ethical hacking engagements and operations.

Embracing Cybersecurity Best Practices

Throughout our journey, we emphasized the importance of adopting cybersecurity best practices, principles, and guidelines to foster a secure, resilient, and trustworthy digital ecosystem. By prioritizing security awareness, education, training, and compliance, and integrating security into the fabric of our organizations, processes, and cultures, we can build robust defenses, mitigate risks, and safeguard our digital assets, infrastructures, and environments against evolving cyber threats and attacks.

Continuous Learning and Professional Development

We concluded our exploration by highlighting the significance of continuous learning and professional development in ethical hacking and cybersecurity. By embracing a lifelong learning mindset, committing to ongoing education, training, and certification, and actively seeking opportunities to expand, refine, and apply our knowledge, skills, and expertise, we can thrive, excel, and make a meaningful and impactful contribution to protecting and defending our digital world.

Ethical hacking is a vital and indispensable discipline in the realm of cybersecurity, empowering us to proactively identify, assess, and mitigate security vulnerabilities and threats, enhance our resilience and readiness against cyber attacks, and safeguard our information, assets, and resources in an increasingly interconnected and digitalized world.

As we move forward, let us continue to embrace the principles, practices, and values of ethical hacking, foster collaboration, cooperation, and communication among cybersecurity professionals, stakeholders, and communities, and champion a culture of security, innovation, and responsibility to create a safer, more secure, and trusted digital future for all.

Thank you for joining us on this enlightening and empowering journey through the fascinating world of ethical hacking. May you continue to explore, learn, grow, and make a positive and lasting impact in the exciting and ever-evolving field of cybersecurity.

Stay Safe. Stay Secure. Happy Hacking!

Let's continue our journey into the captivating realm of cybersecurity, equipping ourselves with the knowledge, skills, and insights to protect and defend against cyber threats effectively, responsibly, and innovatively!